Let's Talk 2

Student's Book

Leo Jones

CAMBRIDGE UNIVERSITY PRESS
Cambridge, New York, Melbourne, Madrid, Cape Town, Singapore, São Paulo

Cambridge University Press
40 West 20th Street, New York, NY 10011–4211, USA

www.cambridge.org
Information on this title: www.cambridge.org/9780521750745

First published 2002
10th printing 2005

Let's Talk Student's Book 2, New Edition, has been developed from
Let's Talk Student's Book, first published by Cambridge University Press in 1996.

Printed in Hong Kong, China

A catalog record of this publication is available from the British Library

Library of Congress Cataloging-in-Publication Data

Jones, Leo, 1943-
Let's talk 1 / Leo Jones.
p. cm.
"Student's book."
ISBN-13 978-0-521-75074-5 Student's Book
ISBN-10 0-521-75074-1 Student's Book
1. English language – Textbooks for foreign speakers. I. Title: Let's talk one.
PE1128 .J624 2002
428.3'4–dc21 2001037375

ISBN-13 978-0-521-75074-5 Student's Book
ISBN-10 0-521-75074-1 Student's Book

Art direction, book design and layout services: Adventure House, NYC

Contents

Author's acknowledgments

Many people contributed their hard work, fresh ideas, helpful encouragement, and sound advice to the *Let's Talk* series.

Thank you to the **reviewers** for their suggestions: Bruce Ballard, Nick Brideson, Steven Brown, Marin Burch, Susan Caesar, Steve Cornwell, Alexandre Figueiredo, Ardis Flenniken, Donna Fujimoto, Aretha Cibele Gaivlat, Sally Gearhart, Sheila Hakner, Christa Hansen, Timothy J. Hogan, Lisa Hori, Madeline Kim, Suzanne Koons, Brian Long, Declan Long, Christopher Lynch, Jackie Maguire, Marie Melenca, Paul Moore, Magali de Moraes Menti, Aphrodite Palavidis, Ane Cibele Palma, Nevitt Reagan, Christine Salica, Rogerio Sanches, Chuck Sandy, Davee Schulte, Benjamin Fenton-Smith, Aviva Smith, and Karen Woolsey.

I would also like to acknowledge the **students** and **teachers** in the following schools and institutes who piloted materials in the initial development stages: **Boston University,** Boston, Massachusetts, U.S.A.; **Center for English Studies,** New York City, New York, U.S.A.; **Centro Cultural Brasil-Estados Unidos,** Belém, Brazil; **Nagasaki Junior College of Foreign Languages,** Nagasaki, Japan; **Nanzen Junior College,** Nagoya, Japan; **Southern Illinois University,** Niigata, Japan; **University of Pittsburgh,** Pittsburgh, Pennsylvania, U.S.A.; **University of Southern California,** Los Angeles, California, U.S.A.

Thanks to the **editorial** and **production team:** Naomi Ben-Shahar, Sylvia P. Bloch, David Bohlke, Patti Brecht, Liane Carita, Ben Clark, Sarah Coleman, Karen Davy, Steve Day, Phyllis Dolgin, Deborah Goldblatt, Nada Gordon, Sandra Graham, Susan Johnson, Rich LePage, James R. Morgan, Kathy Niemczyk, Bill Paulk, Mary Sandre, Howard Siegelman, and Mary Vaughn.

Finally, a special thanks to the Cambridge University Press **staff** and **advisors:** Jim Anderson, Kanako Aoki, Carlos Barbisan, Kathleen Corley, Riitta da Costa, Elizabeth Fuzikava, Steve Golden, Gareth Knight, Nigel McQuitty, Andy Martin, Carine Mitchell, Mark O'Neil, Colin Reublinger, Dan Schulte, Ivan Sorrentino, Ian Sutherland, Koen Van Landeghem, Su-Wei Wang, and Ellen Zlotnick.

To the student

Let's Talk 2 is about communication. It is about listening to and understanding other people's ideas, and about sharing your ideas with your fellow students.

Be brave! Mistakes are an important part of learning. You will make progress, even if you sometimes make a mistake. Your partners and teacher will correct the mistakes that prevent you from communicating effectively.

There are 16 units in *Let's Talk 2*, each containing two lessons. The lessons include these activities:

Pair work and Group work In these activities you can express your ideas and hear the ideas of other students in the class. There are many pair and group work exercises in the book so you will have plenty of speaking practice.

Listening exercises In real life it is necessary to listen carefully in order to understand new information. Each listening exercise in *Let's Talk 2* is accompanied by tasks for you to do as you listen. There are charts to fill in, notes to take, questions to answer, and matching exercises where you choose the right picture for each recording. You can discuss your reaction to the recordings in the pair or group work activities that follow most listenings.

Communication tasks In most units there is a communication task for you to do with a partner or group. Sometimes you will look at photos and decide on a story for the photos. At other times you will share information with a partner or partners. Related communication tasks are on different pages at the back of the book so that you can't read each other's information. The instructions in the lessons tell you which task to look at.

Self-study CD The CD at the back of the book contains many of the recordings used in the classroom. On pages 92 to 107 there are exercises for you to do on your own using the CD. It's best to do these *after* you finish the lesson in class.

Grammar On pages 114 to 121 there are grammar reference pages. These will help to answer any questions you have about grammar.

Let's Talk 2 will help you to enjoy using English while also increasing your vocabulary and improving your grammatical accuracy. But you've read enough for the moment – now, let's talk!

1A What kind of person are you?

Activity 1 **A Pair work** Where are these people? What are they doing? Describe each scene using the words in the box or your own words.

These people are having coffee in a crowded cafe.

B Pair work Which scene do you like most? least? Put the photos in order of preference. Then explain your reasons.

I like the cafe most because I enjoy being around a lot of people.

I'm not interested in the cafe because I don't like noisy places.

C Join another pair Discuss these questions.

- What is your favorite place?
- How do you feel when you are there?
- What do you like about it?

My favorite place is my room. I feel relaxed when I'm there.

Activity 2

A Pair work Look at this list of colors. Choose your favorite color and a color you don't like. Compare with your partner.

black blue brown green pink purple red white yellow

B Pair work Read this chart. Do you and your partner have the personality described for your favorite colors?

WHAT DOES YOUR FAVORITE COLOR SAY ABOUT YOUR PERSONALITY?

BLACK	You are intelligent and love to discuss serious things.
BLUE	You like fresh air and being outdoors, and you like cold weather.
BROWN	You like to be in charge and tell others what to do.
GREEN	You care about the environment and love animals.
PINK	You love to laugh and don't take things too seriously.
PURPLE	You like to be alone and "do your own thing."
RED	You have strong feelings and a quick temper.
WHITE	You love things to be neat and clean, and you always plan ahead.
YELLOW	You are a happy, friendly person, and you love being in the sun.

I like black, and I enjoy discussing serious things.

I like purple, but I don't like to be alone.

C Pair work Discuss these questions.

- Who in your family has a personality similar to yours?
- What other words describe your personality?
- Do you want to change your personality? Why or why not?

My brother is similar to me. He also has a quick temper.

Activity 3

A Pair work You're going to join another pair. First, try to guess the place each person preferred in Activity 1A and his or her favorite color.

Name		
Preferred place		
Favorite color		

B Join another pair Tell the pair your guesses. What do you think each person's favorite place and color tell you about his or her personality?

I think your favorite color is green because you . . .

C Communication task Work with a partner. One of you should look at Task 1 on page 74, and the other at Task 16 on page 80. You're going to interview each other about some of your habits and personal qualities.

1B Breaking the ice

Activity 1

A Pair work Look at the pictures below. Would you want to start a conversation in these situations? Write YES or NO in each box. Explain your reasons.

I'd start a conversation the first week of class. It's important to make friends.

B Pair work "Breaking the ice" means starting a conversation with someone you don't know. Write a good "icebreaker" under the pictures marked YES.

1. It's the first week of class.

....

2. You're stuck in an elevator.

....

3. You see a tourist who needs help.

....

4. A coworker needs help sending a fax.

....

C Listen Compare your ideas with the recording. Was your icebreaker used?

D Listen again Read the questions below. Do you hear these icebreakers? Check (✔) YES or NO. In which conversation do you hear each question? Write the number.

	YES	NO	CONVERSATION #
1. Do you need a hand?	✔		
2. Is this seat taken?			
3. How do you like this class?			
4. Does this happen all the time?			
5. Do you need any help?			
6. Where do you live?			

SELF-STUDY *see page 92*

Activity 2

A Pair work Imagine that you want to start a conversation in each of these situations. What icebreakers would you use?

In the first situation I would ask: "Where do you live?"

B Pair work Write three other situations and possible icebreakers in the chart.

Situation	Icebreaker

C Pair work Choose a situation from the pictures in part A or the chart in part B. Act out the situation using an icebreaker to start the conversation.

Are you new here?

Yes, I just moved here from . . .

D Join another pair Discuss these questions.

- What are some other situations when you would want to start a conversation?
- Do you find it difficult to start a conversation? Why or why not?

I'd start a conversation on the subway.

2A Making a good impression

Activity 1

A Pair work These people are meeting for the first time. Do you think they are making a good impression? Why or why not?

B Pair work Look at these things you might do when you meet a new person for the first time. Check (✔) the things you usually do, and put an X next to the things you never do.

- ☐ shake hands
- ☐ use first names
- ☐ ask what the person's job is
- ☐ buy the person a drink
- ☐ ask how much the person earns
- ☐ look at the person directly
- ☐ smile and laugh a lot
- ☐ bow
- ☐ kiss the person on the cheek
- ☐ find out about the person's interests
- ☐ find out about the person's family
- ☐ exchange business cards
- ☐ touch the person on the arm
- ☐ stand very close
- ☐ hug when you say good-bye
- ☐ put your hands in your pockets and lean against the wall

C Join another pair Compare your greeting habits. Then discuss these questions.

- How are the people in your group alike? How are they different?
- What are some things a visitor to your country should never do?
- Look at the things no one in your group does. Can you think of a country where someone would act this way?

All of us smile and laugh a lot. Only one of us . . .

Activity 2 **A Pair work** Read what the people below say about making good first impressions. Do you agree with the statements?

Glen
"You should worry most about what you say if you want to make a good first impression."

Stacy
"People don't form good first impressions based on how you look. Appearance isn't important."

James
"If you make a poor first impression, it's not difficult to change it to a more positive one."

What you say is very important. People listen closely to what they hear.

I agree it's important, but I think . . . is more important.

B Read/listen First read the article, and try to guess the missing words. Then listen and check your answers.

First Impressions

According to psychologists, people form first impressions based first on how you look, then on how you *sound*, and finally on what you say.

Your physical appearance – how you ________ – makes up 55% of a first impression. This includes facial expressions, body language, and eye contact, as well as ________ and general appearance.

The way you sound makes up ____% of the first impression. This includes how fast or slowly, loudly or softly you ________, and your tone of voice. People listen to your tone of voice and decide whether you sound ________ or unfriendly, interested or bored, and happy or sad. What you say – the actual words you use – counts for only 7% of the message.

People form their first impressions within ____ seconds of meeting you. And first impressions don't change easily. If someone gets the wrong impression of you, it can take a long time to change his or her mind.

Giving a good first impression depends on many things. Everyone ________ in different ways, but when you're not sure you're giving a good impression, the best thing to do is ask yourself, "What would *I* think of someone who acted this way?"

C Group work Imagine you're meeting your group members for the first time. Try to make a good first impression.

D Group work Who made the best first impression? Why?

2B Getting personal

Activity 1

A Pair work Read these sentences. Which might you use in a conversation with a stranger?

Did you see the game last night?

Can you believe this weather? It's awful.

What do you do for a living?

It's nice to meet you.
I've heard so much about you.

What do you do in your free time?

Tell me about yourself.

I like your jacket.
Where did you get it?

How do you like school?

How do you like the party?
Are you having a good time?

You look familiar.
Have we met before?

B Pair work Imagine you are meeting these people for the first time. Write one question you might ask each person. Then discuss the questions below.

People	Questions
a classmate	
a teacher	
a possible employer	
a neighbor	
your brother's girlfriend	
your sister's boyfriend	
your future mother-in-law	
your future father-in-law	

- What questions would be inappropriate to ask the people in the chart?
- Which person would you be most comfortable meeting? most uncomfortable? Why?

It would be inappropriate to ask a teacher his or her age.

C Pair work Role-play possible meetings with the people in part B.

So, do you like this class so far?

Yes, it's very interesting. How about you?

Activity 2 **A Listen** A reporter is interviewing Michael and Amy. First read the questions below. Then listen and write the answers.

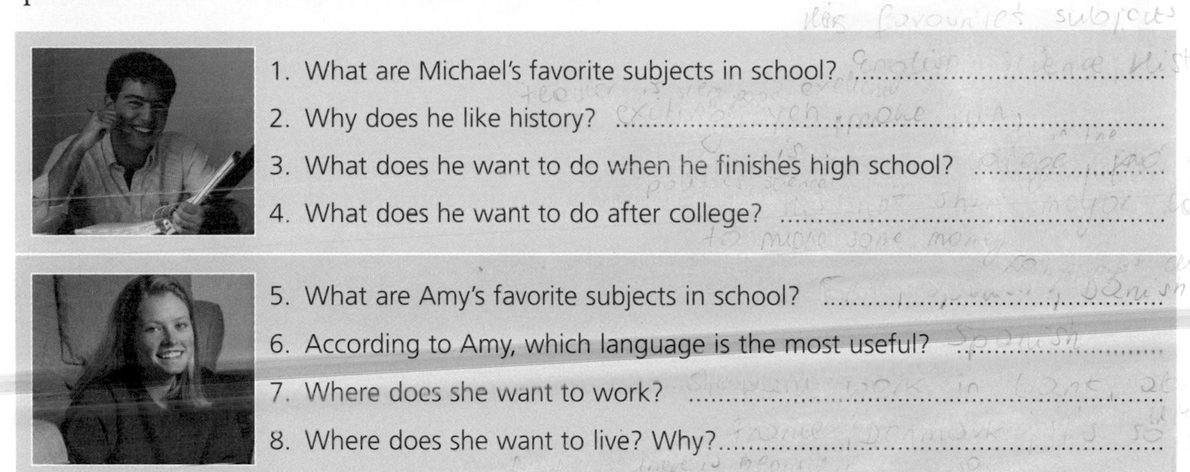

1. What are Michael's favorite subjects in school?
2. Why does he like history?
3. What does he want to do when he finishes high school?
4. What does he want to do after college?
5. What are Amy's favorite subjects in school?
6. According to Amy, which language is the most useful?
7. Where does she want to work?
8. Where does she want to live? Why?

B Listen again Write five questions the interviewer asks Michael. Then write five things the interviewer says to encourage Amy to say more.

Interview with Michael	**Interview with Amy**
Questions:	***Encouraging sounds and phrases:***
What's your favorite class?	*Uh-huh*

C Pair work Compare your notes. Are you more similar to Michael or Amy?

Activity 3 **A Work alone** Write five questions you could ask someone you have just met.

B Pair work Ask your partner questions to find out more about him or her.

What kind of music do you like?

I like classical. I don't like . . .

C Join another pair Tell your group members something you learned about your partner.

Lucy likes classical music, but she doesn't like pop.

D Communication task Work in groups of three. One of you should look at Task 2 on page 74, one at Task 17 on page 80, and one at Task 31 on page 86. You're going to find out more about your classmates.

SELF-STUDY *see page 93*

3A How do you cook that?

Activity 1 **A Work alone** Fill out this chart about your favorite foods. Then compare with a partner. Tell each other why you like the things you do.

What's your favorite . . . ?

main dish		dessert	
vegetable		snack	
beverage		ethnic food	

What do you like to cook?

What's your "specialty"?

What's your favorite restaurant?

My favorite snack is potato chips. I love salty foods.

B Join another pair Compare your answers. Then discuss these questions.

- What's your least favorite in each category of the chart?
- What foods bring back your best memories?

My least favorite beverage is coffee. *I don't like milk at all.*

C Group work Circle the words below that you don't know, and ask your group to explain them. Use a dictionary to look up any that none of you knows. Then add two more items to each list.

Ways of preparing food	peel slice stir beat whip marinate
Ways of cooking	fry deep-fry broil grill bake steam melt roast
Equipment	frying pan skillet roasting pan pot oven burner steamer

Activity 2

A Listen Three people are describing their favorite dishes. Check (✔) the ingredients in each recipe.

Recipe 1	Recipe 2	Recipe 3
☐ one flounder	☐ chicken pieces	☐ flour
☐ soy sauce	☐ garlic salt	☐ salt
☐ garlic	☐ garlic powder	☐ milk
☐ scallions	☐ thyme	☐ cream
☐ ginger slices	☐ oregano	☐ water
☐ vegetable oil	☐ seasoned salt	☐ eggs
☐ rice	☐ peanut oil	☐ butter

B Listen again Complete the instructions with the missing words.

1. Steamed flounder with ginger and scallions

1. Marinate the *flounder* in soy sauce overnight.
2. ________ the fish for three to four minutes.
3. Place scallions and ________ on top of the fish, and steam for three or four more minutes.
4. Then pour hot ________ over the flounder and serve.

2. "Mama Pearl's double-seasoned fried chicken"

1. Season the chicken pieces.
2. Then fill a ________ paper ________ halfway with flour and seasoning.
3. Put the chicken pieces inside the bag, close the top, and ________.
4. Then fry the chicken in a ________ until the pieces are brown.
5. ________ the chicken on a brown paper bag and serve.

3. Yorkshire pudding

1. Take one cup of ________, half a teaspoon of ________, half a cup of milk, ________ ________ of water, and two eggs.
2. ________ the ingredients together until the mixture is smooth.
3. Rub a little oil onto a baking pan, and put it in the ________ until it gets hot.
4. Take it out and pour the ________ into the pan.
5. Then ________ in the oven for thirty minutes. Serve with roast beef.

C Pair work Compare your answers. Then discuss these questions.

- Which dish sounds the most delicious? the least delicious?
- Which dish do you think is the easiest to make? the hardest?

D Pair work Explain how to prepare a dish that is popular in your family.

We often make hash brown potatoes. First you peel and slice some . . .

E Join another pair Exchange recipes. Which dishes would you like to try?

SELF-STUDY *see page 94*

3B Going out to eat

Activity 1

A Pair work Imagine that you're sitting together in a restaurant. Read this menu and decide what you want to order.

MENU

APPETIZERS

Shrimp cocktail
shrimp on a bed of lettuce with a tasty sauce

Fresh asparagus
served with melted butter

MAIN DISHES

T-bone steak
broiled and served with french fries and vegetable of the day

Spaghetti and meatballs
homemade pasta in tomato sauce, served with a green salad

Vegetarian plate
a selection of grilled vegetables served with rice or a baked potato

Fajitas
slices of steak grilled with green peppers and onions, served with hot tortillas

Tempura
fresh seafood and vegetables dipped in egg batter and deep-fried

Caesar salad
lettuce with a dressing of anchovies, eggs, and cheese, served with hot French bread

DESSERTS

Homemade ice cream
chocolate, vanilla, strawberry, coffee

Banana split
giant banana with ice cream, nuts, chocolate syrup, and whipped cream

Homemade apple pie
served with vanilla ice cream or whipped cream

Tropical fruit salad
a generous selection of papaya, mangoes, and pineapple

Special today! Two-for-one offer!
Two people ordering exactly the same items from the menu pay for just ONE meal.
(Drinks and tip extra)

What are you going to have?

I feel like having something light. Maybe I'll try . . .

B Join another pair Imagine that you see some friends sitting at another table. Join them and sit together. Explain what you have decided to order.

C Group work Now you notice the "two-for-one" offer at the bottom of the menu. Decide whether you want to change your minds about your orders.

D Group work Suggest some dishes for someone who:

can't eat meat	loves fried food	hopes to lose weight
doesn't like red meat	wants a healthy dessert	is extremely hungry

Someone who can't eat meat can have the asparagus, the vegetarian plate, or . . .

Activity 2 **A Pair work** Look at the pictures. What do you think each person is saying? Write your guess.

B Listen Now you will hear the six conversations. Did you guess correctly?

C Group work Discuss these questions.

- What kinds of restaurants do you like? What kinds don't you like?
- How often do you go out to eat? Who do you usually go with?
- What's the best meal you've ever had in a restaurant?

I really enjoy going to family restaurants. I don't like . . .

Activity 3 **A Group work** Work in groups of three. Write a menu with typical dishes from different parts of your country, or write an international menu with dishes from different countries.

B Communication task Work with your same group. One person in your group should look at Task 3 on page 75, and the other two at Task 18 on page 81. You're going to ask and answer questions about the menu you wrote.

4A Families

Activity 1 **A Pair work** Review the meaning of these words. Then discuss the questions below.

grandmother	daughter	sister	wife	niece
mother	granddaughter	sister-in-law	aunt	cousin

- What's the masculine equivalent of the words?
- In your language, do you have a single word to describe each of the people?

B Pair work Look at the family tree below. Explain how James is related to the other people in the chart.

James is Karen's husband. James and Karen are Jessica's parents.

C Listen Alice is discussing these people in her family. Draw her family tree on a separate piece of paper.

Bill	Carol	Doug	Ellen	Frank
Gina	Henry	Irene	Jack	Kumiko

D Work alone Draw your own family tree.

E Pair work Explain "who is who" in your family.

Activity 2 **A Pair work** Look at these photos. How do you think the people in each picture are related to each other?

I think these people are the little girl's parents. The other two people are her . . .

B Work alone What are some advantages and disadvantages of living with your parents until you're married? Complete the chart.

Advantages	Disadvantages
can save money	*not enough privacy*

C Group work Compare your ideas.

An advantage of living with your parents is that you can save money.

That's true. A disadvantage is not having enough privacy.

D Group work Discuss these questions.

- How has family life in your country changed since your parents were your age?
- What is a "typical" family in your country?

When my parents were my age, they used to . . .

4B Friends

Activity 1 **Pair work** Look at these photos of friends. Then discuss the questions below.

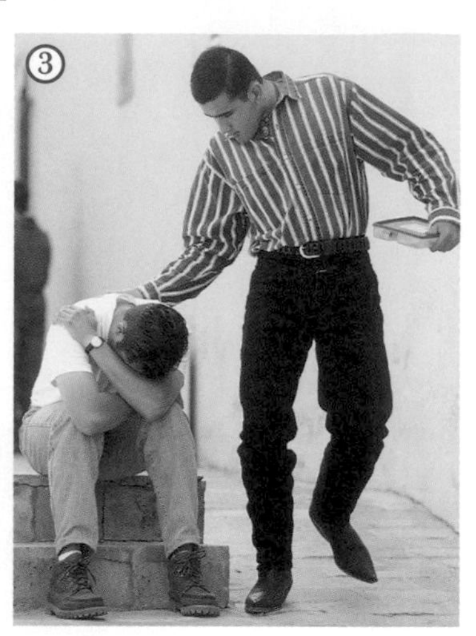

- What's happening in each picture?
- What do you think has just happened? What do you think will happen next?

The woman doesn't seem to like what her friend is saying.

Activity 2 **A Listen** Three people are talking about their friends. Write one reason why they get along well with each friend and one thing they do together. ✻

	Why they get along	What they do together
Tom's old friend Jeff	*share a lot of interests*	
Tom's new friend Erica		
Lori's old friend Steven		
Lori's new friend Mary		
Phyllis's old friend Dorothy		

B Group work Compare your answers. Then discuss these questions.

- Who is your best friend? How did you first meet?
- Who is your newest friend? How did you meet?
- Why would you stop being friends with someone? Give some reasons.

My best friend is Anita. We first met in elementary school.

✻ SELF-STUDY *see page 95*

C Listen Tom, Lori, and Phyllis are answering the question: "Why are friends important to you?" Take notes on their answers.

Tom	*you don't feel alone*
Lori	
Phyllis	

D Pair work Compare your notes. Who do you agree with most: Tom, Lori, or Phyllis?

Activity 3

A Group work Look at the list below. Which things do you expect a good friend to do for you? Which things do you do for a friend?

take the blame for something you did	travel across the city to see you
write you a letter every week	lend you money
pay for you in a restaurant	let you win a game against him/her
listen to your problems	remember your birthday
phone you every day	give you advice
tell the truth, even if it hurts	send you flowers
keep a secret	not talk behind your back
not hold a grudge	be a friend when times are rough

I expect a good friend to listen to my problems and keep a secret.

Yes, and I never hold a grudge against a friend.

B Communication task Work with a partner. One of you should look at Task 4 on page 75, and the other at Task 19 on page 81. Each of you is going to choose someone you would like to be friends with. Their pictures are below.

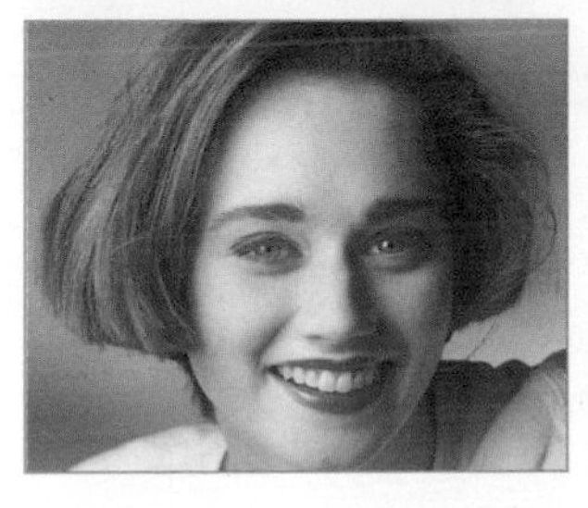

Review puzzles

Puzzle A

Use the clues to complete the puzzle with words from Unit 1.

Across

1. the opposite of "interesting"
2. If you like this color, you may like to be alone.
3. Someone who likes black is .... .
4. Someone who likes white likes to plan .... .
5. He gets angry easily. He has a .... temper.
6. the opposite of "shy"
7. Who in your family has a .... similar to yours?
8. Do you like to be in .... and tell others what to do?
9. The place wasn't crowded – it was almost .... .
10. I like her even though she has some strange .... .
11. not noisy
12. What are your best personal .... ?
13. On Fridays I wear .... clothes at work.
14. She isn't a messy person. She's very .... .

Down

15. Making contact with someone for the first time is known as ....

Puzzle B

1. Here are 4 scrambled phrases. Unscramble the letters to make phrases from Lesson 2A.

a baggy nodule — b___ l_______
cat yet once — e__ c______
fiasco explainers — f______ e________
search pay appliance — p______ a__________

2. Here are 4 more scrambled phrases. Unscramble the letters to make phrases from Lesson 2B.

ape crushing orange — e__________ p_____
at fur objectives — f_______ s________
meet fire — f___ t___
proper piano quantities — i_____________ q_______

3. Now use the letters in the circles above to complete the sentence.

"Always try to make a good first _ _ _ _ _ _ _ _ _ _ _ _ _ _ _ _ _."

Puzzle C

There are 25 words from Unit 3 in this word search puzzle. How many can you find? They all have something to do with FOOD.

Puzzle D

Use the clues to solve the puzzle with words from Unit 4.

Across

4. If you live with your parents, it's hard to get any .... .
8. the opposite of "feminine"
9. They have two sons and one .... .
10. My .... is: Live for today!
12. They got engaged in July but aren't getting .... until December.
13. Tom Brown is Mrs. Brown's .... .
15. Your sister's son is your .... .

Down

1. Your mother's father is your .... .
2. He has held a .... against me for a long time.
3. Your sister's husband is your ....-in-law.
5. Your aunt's son is your .... .
6. Your .... tree shows how all your relatives are related.
7. Would you ever take the .... for something a friend did wrong?
11. I have a problem. Can you give me some .... ?
14. Your brother's daughter is your .... .

5A Nine to five

Activity 1

A Pair work Look at these photos. What is each person's job? What would you enjoy about each job?

He's a construction worker. Some of the things I'd enjoy about his job are working outside and . . .

B Pair work Circle the words below that you don't know, and ask your partner to explain them. Use a dictionary to look up any that neither of you knows. Then add the words to the chart.

boss
employee
employer
freelance position
full-time job
health insurance
hourly wages
manager
office worker
overtime pay
part-time job
pay
raise
retirement plan
supervisor
temporary position

People's roles at work	Salary and benefits	Job types
boss	health insurance	freelance position

C Join another pair What do the people in your family do for a living? What do you think they like or dislike about their jobs?

My mother is a manager in a bank. She likes the pay, but she doesn't like . . .

Activity 2 **A Listen** Laura and Christopher are talking to their bosses on the first day of their new jobs. Check (✔) the duties they're told about. Then write the hours they work.

Laura works from .... to ....

Christopher works from .... to ....

B Pair work Compare your answers. What would you enjoy about each job?

C Listen Laura and Christopher are now discussing what they enjoyed about their first day of work. Check (✔) the things each person mentions.

Laura	Christopher
☐ a large company	☐ not very complicated
☐ a supportive boss	☐ friendly people
☐ good overtime pay	☐ free juice
☐ a future raise	☐ a quiet lunch hour

Activity 3 **Group work** Discuss these questions.

- Tell about a job you've had. What did you do? What did you like and dislike about the job?
- What kind of job do you think you'll have 5 years from now? 30 years from now?
- What's your ideal job? Give your reasons.
- What job benefits are important to you?
- What's your idea of a terrible job?

I had a part-time job last summer as a waiter in a coffee shop. I really liked it because I only worked . . .

SELF-STUDY *see page 96*

5B The movie industry

Activity 1

A Pair work Can you guess what these people in the movie industry do? Match the jobs to the photos. Then turn to page 89 to check your answers.

a. cameraperson
b. stuntperson
c. makeup artist
d. animal trainer
e. film editor
f. grip

1

2

3

4

5

6

B Communication task Work in groups of three. One of you should look at Task 5 on page 75, one at Task 20 on page 81, and one at Task 32 on page 86. You're going to find out more about the jobs above.

C Group work Which jobs in part A would you enjoy? not enjoy? Why?

I'd enjoy being an animal trainer. I love animals.

I wouldn't enjoy that. I'm not a very patient person.

Activity 2 **A Read/listen** First read the magazine article, and try to guess the missing words. Then listen and check your answers.

Walking for a Living

A Foley artist earns a living adding sounds like footsteps to movie sound tracks. Footsteps are added in sound studios because when a movie is filmed, the ________ are aimed at the actors' mouths, not their ________ – and because real footsteps just don't sound natural.

Foley artists also add all kinds of sound effects to movies. In a horror film, the sound of ________ breaking is made by snapping celery and dry spaghetti. The sound of burning bodies is created by dripping water onto a hot iron. The sound of horses' hooves used to be made using ________, but modern Foley artists prefer to use a toilet plunger. The sound of ________-________ is made by scraping an ax across concrete – real ice doesn't sound natural enough.

Most Foley artists are very private people. Their work is done in special sound studios, and they don't appear in front of the public or even in front of the ________. And they don't get the appreciation they deserve – if they do the job right, the ________ doesn't even notice.

A Foley artist at work

B Pair work How do you think a Foley artist creates these sounds? Check (✔) your guesses. Then turn to page 89 to check your answers.

1. a bird flying
   - ☐ waving a notebook
   - ☐ opening and closing an umbrella
2. boiling water
   - ☐ pouring water onto the floor
   - ☐ blowing through a straw into water
3. writing
   - ☐ scratching paper with a paper clip
   - ☐ rolling a stone in a jar
4. walking in the snow
   - ☐ squeezing a balloon
   - ☐ squeezing a bag of flour

C Pair work Discuss these questions.

- In the movie industry, would you prefer to work "behind the scenes" or in front of the camera?
- What are the advantages to having a job besides money and benefits?
- If you were rich, would you still want a job? Why or why not?

I'd prefer to work behind the scenes as a director.

Really? I think being an actor would be more interesting.

6A What do you enjoy doing?

Activity 1 **A Pair work** What are the leisure activities shown in these pictures? Which of them do you enjoy doing? Why?

I enjoy bicycling and walking because I like to be outdoors.

B Listen Three people are talking about their favorite leisure activities. As you listen, complete the first column of the chart with the activities pictured in part A.

		Favorite hobbies or interests	What do you enjoy most about each activity?	How long do you spend on each activity?
Wanda	1.	*walking*		
	2.			
Robert	1.			
	2.			
Christopher	1.			
	2.			

C Listen again What do the people enjoy most about the activities, and how much time do they spend on them? Complete the second and third columns of the chart above.

D Group work Who would you like to spend some free time with: Wanda, Robert, or Christopher? Why?

SELF-STUDY *see page 97*

Activity 2 **A Pair work** Look at the photos. Then discuss the questions below.

taking photographs

doing puzzles

snorkeling

jogging

playing video games

bowling

- Do you do any of the activities? Which ones?
- Which activity looks like the most fun? the least fun?

B Pair work Which of your interests gives you the most enjoyment? Explain why you enjoy it so much.

I love playing tennis. I enjoy it because it's great exercise and . . .

C Group work Discuss these questions.

- What is something you were once interested in, but aren't anymore? What happened?
- If you had time for only one of your hobbies or interests, which one would you choose? Why?

I used to play computer games, but I don't have enough time anymore.

D Communication task Work with a partner. One of you should look at Task 6 on page 76, and the other at Task 21 on page 82. You're going to talk about some more activities.

6B If I had more time . . .

Activity 1 **A Pair work** If a lifetime could be compressed into a week, this is how much time a person would spend doing these things. Look at the chart. Then discuss the questions below.

A person would spend . . .

120 hours	at home	14 hours	eating	6 hours	in school and college
60 hours	in bed	12 hours	waiting in line	5 hours	on hobbies and interests
24 hours	at work	12 hours	shopping	3 hours	traveling
16 hours	in the bathroom	10 hours	cleaning house	1 hour	waiting at red lights
14 hours	watching TV	7 hours	in meetings	½ hour	in movie theaters

- Which statistics are surprising or unbelievable?
- How do you generally spend your leisure time?
- If you had more leisure time, how would you spend it?

I'm surprised a person spends 12 hours waiting in line. I can't believe that.

B Work alone Look at these common chores. Check (✔) the ones that you do.

___ pay bills	___ clean	___ take out the garbage
___ wash the dishes	___ do laundry	___ feed a pet
___ shop for groceries	___ recycle things at home	___ return books or videos

C Pair work Look at the chores in part B again, and discuss these questions.

- Which chore do you dislike doing the most? Why?
- Are there any chores you enjoy doing? Which ones?
- What other chores do you do?

I hate shopping for groceries because there's always a long line of people.

Activity 2 **A Work alone** Read the items in the chart. Then add three more leisure activities that you like to do.

How many times did you . . . ?

	You	Your partner		You	Your partner
watch a sports game	....	....	go to a cafe	....	....
play a sport	....	....	read a book	....	....
play cards	....	....	read a magazine	....	....
play a computer game	....	....	listen to music	....	....
watch a video	....	....	go shopping	....	....
watch television	....	....	eat out	....	....
go to the movies	....	....	prepare a meal	....	....
go for a walk	....	....	....	....	....
visit a museum	....	....	....	....	....
go dancing	....	....	....	....	....

B Pair work Approximately how many times did you and your partner do the activities in part A in the past month? Complete the chart.

How many times did you watch a sports game?

Let's see. I think about six times. How about you?

C Join another pair Compare your leisure activities. Then discuss these questions.

- In what ways are you the same? different?
- Who do you think has the most leisure time? the least?
- Who do you think spends their leisure time most productively? Why?

We both go dancing a lot.

You eat out more often than I do.

D Group work Think of a leisure activity you haven't done recently. Imagine you're completely free this weekend. Tell about what you're going to do.

I love going to baseball games, so I'm going to see my favorite team play.

7A Playing and watching sports

Activity 1 **A Pair work** Look at these photos. Then discuss the questions below.

- Are these sports popular in your country? Do you play any of them?
- What's the most popular sport in your country? the most popular sports team?
- What do you think is the most exciting sport? the most boring?
- What do you think is the most dangerous sport? Why?
- Do you like to play sports? Why or why not?

Baseball is very popular, but I don't play it.

B Listen Six people are talking about what they do to stay in shape. Write one advantage for the healthy practice each person mentions.

	Advantages
1. Lori does yoga.	*calming*
2. Terry goes swimming.	
3. Robert runs.	
4. Trevor walks everywhere.	
5. Christopher plays basketball.	
6. Bill follows a vegetarian diet.	

SELF-STUDY *see page 98*

C Pair work Compare your answers. Then discuss these questions.

- Of the six people you heard in part B, whose ideas do you agree with most? Why?
- Whose ideas do you agree with the least? Why?
- What do you do to keep healthy and stay in shape?

I agree with Robert. Running is good for your whole body.

Activity 2

A Pair work Look at the sports listed below. Which of the sports follow the word *play*? the word *go*? the word *do*? Write *play, go,* or *do* next to each sport. Then turn to page 89 to check your answers.

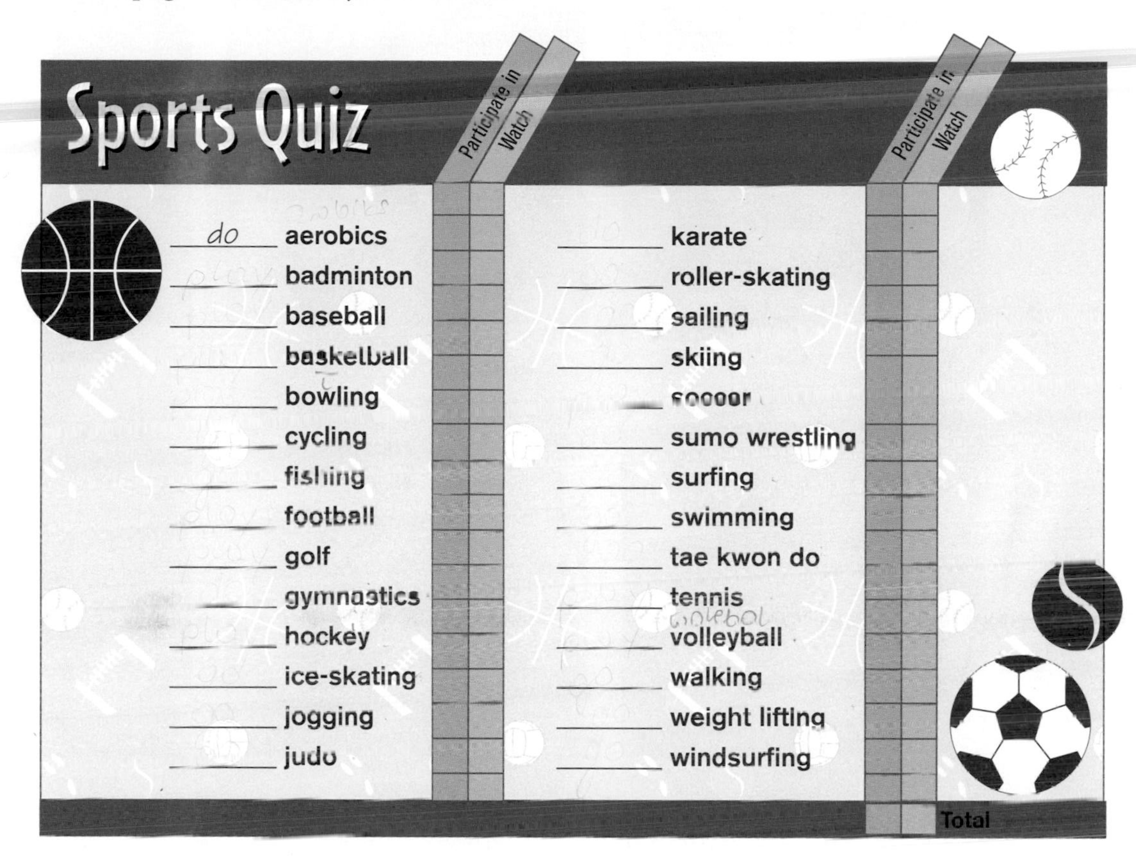

Sports Quiz

	Sport	Participate in	Watch		Sport	Participate in	Watch
do	aerobics			______	karate		
______	badminton			______	roller-skating		
______	baseball			______	sailing		
______	basketball			______	skiing		
______	bowling			______	soccer		
______	cycling			______	sumo wrestling		
______	fishing			______	surfing		
______	football			______	swimming		
______	golf			______	tae kwon do		
______	gymnastics			______	tennis		
______	hockey			______	volleyball		
______	ice-skating			______	walking		
______	jogging			______	weight lifting		
______	judo			______	windsurfing		
					Total		

B Pair work Are you a "sports nut"? Follow these instructions to find out.

1. How many times a year do you participate in each sport? Write the number in the *Participate in* columns of the quiz.
2. How many times a year do you watch other people participate in each sport? Write the number in the *Watch* columns of the quiz.
3. Add up all the numbers in the *Participate in* columns of the quiz.
4. Add up all the numbers in the *Watch* columns of the quiz.

C Pair work Turn to page 89 to find out what your score means. Then discuss these questions.

- Is the quiz right about you? How much of a "sports nut" do *you* think you are?
- Which of your favorite sports are missing from the list?

I think the quiz is right. I really am a sports nut!

7B How about a game?

Activity 1 **A Pair work** Look at these different types of games. Are they popular in your country? Which have you played?

chess | solitaire | mah-jongg

hangman | charades | Tetris

Mah-jongg is popular with some people, but I've never played it.

B Pair work What games are well known in your country? Write down as many examples as you can.

board games	
card games	
tile games	
word games	
party games	
computer games	

C Join another pair Discuss these questions.

- What games do you like to play?
- What game would you like to learn how to play? Why?
- What games did you play as a child, but don't play now?

I like to play card games sometimes.

Activity 2

A Group work Read these descriptions of some popular word games. Then choose one game to play in your group.

"I went on a trip . . ."

Each player has to remember the list of things started by the previous player and add one more item to the list.

For example:
A: I went on a trip and took an umbrella.
B: I went on a trip and took an umbrella and a guidebook.
C: I went on a trip and took an umbrella, a guidebook, and my sister.

The first player who makes a mistake has to start a new list.

"Who am I?"

One person leaves the room. The others in the group think of a famous person – real or fictional, living or dead. The person who left the room returns and asks, "Who am I?" Each person in the group has to answer the question with a clue.

For example:
A: Who am I?
B: You're a movie star.
A: Who am I?
C: You're very good-looking.
A: Who am I?
D: You have blond hair.

When each person in the group has answered, the person guessing has three chances to guess the famous person. If he or she is wrong, the others give the correct answer. Then another person leaves the room, and the game begins again.

Endings and beginnings

One player says a word. The next player has to say a word beginning with the letter that ended the previous word.

For example:
A: apple
B: elephant
C: tomato
D: only

If the next player can't think of a word or gets the letter wrong, he or she is out of the game. The winner is the last one to give a correct word.

Word associations

One player says a word. Then, without hesitating, the next player has to say another word that the first word brings to mind. If someone hesitates (or says a word that is not associated in any way), he or she drops out. The game continues until just one player is left.

For example:
A: vacation
B: photograph
C: camera
D: movie
E: star
F: sun

B Group work Choose a second game to play. Then compare your experiences with the rest of the class. Which games did you like the most? Why?

C Communication task Work in groups of three. One of you should look at Task 7 on page 76, one at Task 22 on page 82, and one at Task 33 on page 86. Each of you is going to read about and explain another word game.

8A Going places

Activity 1 **A Pair work** Look at what these people did on their vacations. Which vacations look like fun? Which don't?

The camping vacation looks like a lot of fun because I love sleeping outdoors.

B Listen Four people are describing their vacations. Write the number of the description on the correct picture in part A.

C Listen again Who is describing his or her vacation? Check (✔) the correct box.

Who . . . ?	*Wanda*	*Robert*	*Marni*	*Tom*
didn't miss his/her family				
didn't enjoy doing the chores				
expected to be bored – but wasn't				
went to the zoo				
got wet and scared				
missed his/her friends				
picked fruit				
enjoyed watching the stars				
studied				
thinks the country is too quiet				
walked 200 miles in a week				
went jogging or swimming every day				
went to the opera				
wishes he/she had planned ahead better				

SELF-STUDY *see page 99*

D Pair work Compare your answers. Then discuss these questions.

- Now that you know more about what the people did on their vacations, would you answer the questions in part A differently? Why?
- What's the nicest vacation you have taken? Tell your partner about it.

Robert's vacation sounded really nice. It's fun to show people your hometown.

Activity 2 **A Group work** Look at these photos. Then discuss the questions below.

- What are the people doing? Where do you think they are?
- Imagine that you can take one of these vacations. Which one would you choose? Why?
- If your dream vacation isn't shown here, describe it to the group.

B Communication task Work with a partner. One of you should look at Task 8 on page 76, and the other at Task 23 on page 82. You're going to look at some vacation snapshots.

8B On the road

Activity 1 **A Pair work** Imagine you're the people in these photos. What would you do in each situation?

I would lock the car and go look for help.

I wouldn't. I'd wait for someone to stop.

B Pair work Look at the chart. Then discuss the questions below.

KILOMETERS Traveled per Person per Year

	by car	by train	by air
Brazil	3,600	110	185
France	10,400	1,131	919
Japan	4,400	1,923	746
South Korea	2,311	698	428
United Kingdom	10,100	583	1,845
United States	16,400	80	2,775

1.6 kilometers = 1 mile

- In which country do people travel the most by car? by train? by air? In which country do people travel the least by these forms of transportation?
- What do you think are the reasons for the differences?
- What forms of transportation do you use? Where do you take them?

People travel the most by car in the United States.

C Join another pair Tell the group how you get to class. Who has the easiest trip? the most difficult? Who takes more than one form of transportation?

Activity 2

A Pair work Think about where you are right now. What's the best way to get to these places?

the nearest airport	the nearest post office	the nearest stadium
the nearest park	the nearest beach	the nearest country

The best way to get to the airport is by car.

Actually, it's easier and cheaper to go by bus.

B Pair work Look at the photos. Then discuss the questions below.

a family sedan

a sports-utility vehicle (an SUV)

a sports car

a classic car

a limousine

a jeep

- Do you think a car says something about its driver? What kind of person typically drives each of the cars above?
- What kinds of cars are the most popular in your country?
- Which car above would you like to have? Why?

I think single people typically drive sports cars.

C Join another pair Have you ever taken driving lessons? a driving test? Describe the experience.

Review puzzles

Puzzle A

Use the clues to complete the puzzle with words from Unit 5.

Across

1. the money a worker is paid
2. He asked his boss for a .... .
3. A .... artist adds sound effects to movies.
4. She has a .... position. She's not directly employed.
5. extra pay for working extra hours
6. someone who works for a company
7. .... paper with a paper clip to make the sound of writing.
8. I'm not very .... . I hate waiting in lines, for example.
9. What is your .... job?
10. .... through a straw into water to make the sound of boiling water.
11. .... a bag of flour to make the sound of walking in snow.
12. After working for 40 years, she's looking forward to .... .
13. His current job is only .... , not permanent.
14. She has a ....-time job. She works 40 hours a week.
15. Have you ever had a part-.... job?
16. My boss is friendly and .... .
17. If you want to leave work early, ask your .... .

Down

18. the money you're paid, plus extra advantages, such as health insurance

Puzzle B

1. Here are 6 scrambled words. Unscramble the letters to make words from Lesson 6A.

ivyattic	a c t i v (i) t y
metojenny	e _ _ _ _ _ _ _ _ _
ecriesxe	e _ _ _ _ _ ( ) _
bhboy	h _ _ _ _
zuplez	p _ _ _ _ _
resentit	i _ _ _ _ ( ) _ _

2. Here are 6 more scrambled words. Unscramble the letters to make words from Lesson 6B.

runlady	l a (u) n d r y
orche	c _ _ _ ( )
pingposh	s _ _ _ _ _ _ _
lancegin	c ( ) _ _ _ _ _ _ _
abeggar	g _ ( ) _ _ _ _
ravngitel	t _ _ _ _ _ _ _ _

3. Now use the letters in the circles above to complete the sentence.

"Do you have much _ _ _ _ _ _ _ _ time?"

Puzzle C

There are 24 words from Unit 7 in this word search puzzle. How many can you find? They all have something to do with SPORTS and GAMES.

Puzzle D

Use the clues to solve the puzzle with words from Unit 8.

Across

1. There's only room for one passenger in his .... car.
5. Where are you going on .... this summer?
7. It's fun to show visitors around your .... .
9. I didn't want to take a suitcase, so I took a .... instead.
10. An SUV is a sports-.... vehicle.
11. Don't forget to .... your car.
12. *Madama Butterfly* is a famous .... by Puccini.
14. We enjoyed looking at their vacation .... .
15. a very big, luxurious car
16. He says his 1973 Mercedes is a .... car, but I think it's just an old wreck.

Down

1. A family .... has plenty of room in the back for passengers.
2. Cars, buses, and trains are forms of .... .
3. You can see wild animals here.
4. In a city you can watch sports events in a .... .
6. They like sleeping .... under the stars.
8. a longer word for "car"
13. You need a tent if you're going .... .

9A What's it like there?

Activity 1 **A Pair work** Look at these photos. Describe each one using the words in the box or your own words.

In the first picture, there's a sailboat on the water. The skyscrapers are . . .

B Pair work Which country or countries do you think the photos in part A show?

C Join another pair Turn to page 90 to check your answer. Then discuss these questions.

- Have you ever visited another country? What did you like about it? What did you dislike?
- If you could visit another country, where would you go? Why?

I went to Brazil last summer. I enjoyed the beaches and . . .

Activity 2 **A Listen** Jackie, Nick, and Kate are talking about countries they have visited. First read the questions below. Then listen and write the answers. Guess which country each person is talking about.

① **Jackie**

1. What was the weather like? ....
2. What did she like the most about her trip? ....
3. What was her favorite place? Why? ....
4. What country do you think Jackie is talking about? ....

② **Nick**

1. What did Nick do during the first part of his trip? ....
2. What did he like the most about his trip? ....
3. Why would he go back? ....
4. What country do you think Nick is talking about? ....

③ **Kate**

1. What was the weather like? ....
2. What did Kate like the most about her trip? ....
3. What did she buy in Taxco? ....
4. What country do you think Kate is talking about? ....

B Pair work Which place in part A would you like to visit the most? Why?

C Group work Discuss these questions.

- What are the most popular tourist attractions in your country?
- What cities or regions in your country do most tourists visit? Would you tell a visitor to your country to go there? Why or why not?
- What can a tourist do to get a really authentic experience in your country?

The most popular tourist attractions are the museums and temples.

SELF-STUDY *see page 100*

9B Before you go

Activity 1 **A Pair work** Which of these things do you think can be found in New Zealand?

beaches	glaciers	rivers
caves	lakes	sand dunes
fjords	meadows	volcanoes
forests	mountains	wilderness

I think New Zealand has beaches, mountains, forests, and . . .

B Pair work Turn to page 90 to check your answers.

C Read/listen First read the advertisement, and try to guess the missing words. Then listen and check your answers.

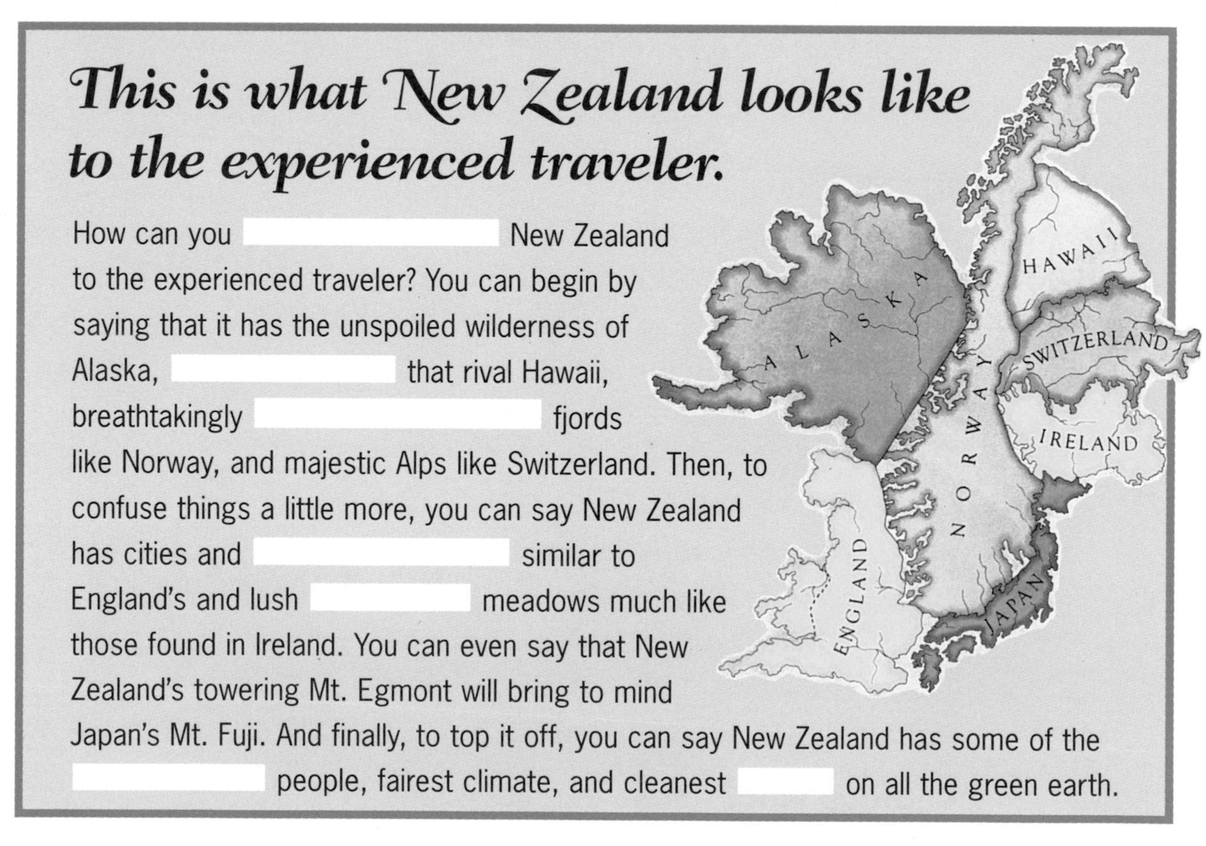

D Pair work Compare your answers. Then discuss these questions.

- How is New Zealand similar to your country? How is it different?
- What would you most like to see in New Zealand?

My country has high mountains and green meadows, but we don't have beaches.

Activity 2 **A Pair work** Look at the pictures. Then match each item in the box with the correct picture.

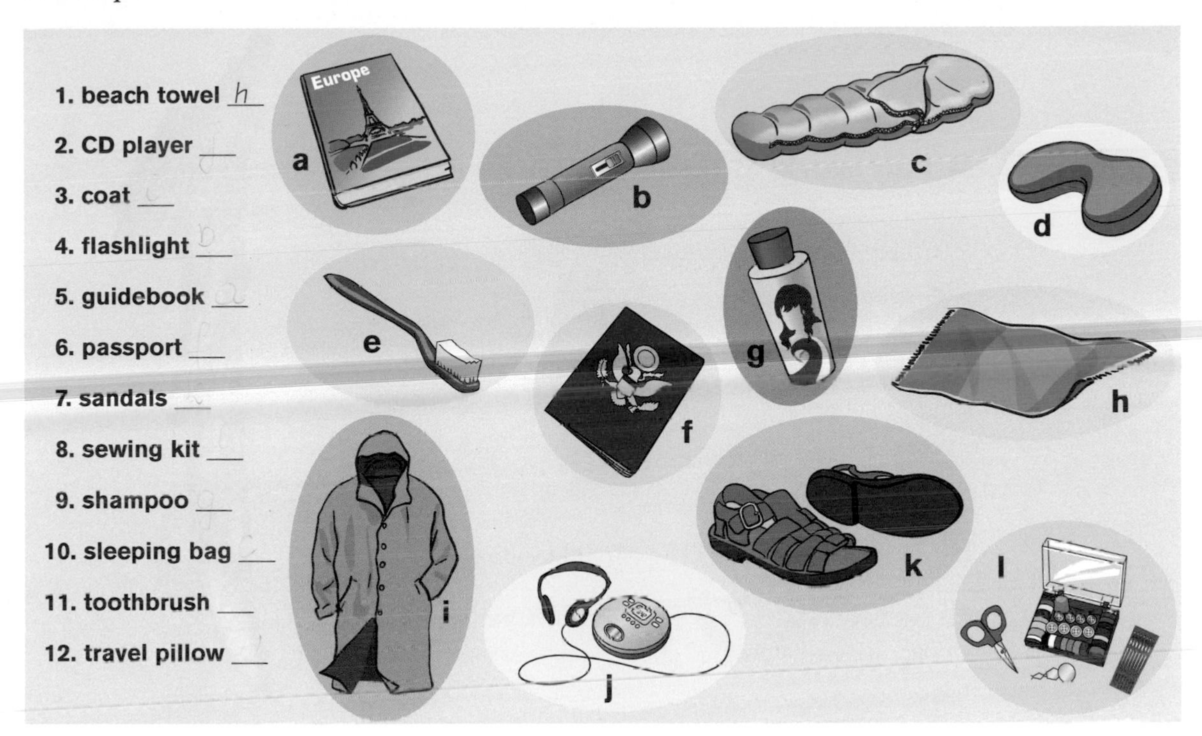

B Pair work Compare answers. Then turn to page 90 to check your answers.

C Pair work Which items would you be sure to take with you on . . . ?

an overnight camping trip　　a day trip to the beach　　a trip overseas

For an overnight camping trip, we'd need sleeping bags.

We'd also need a flashlight and . . .

D Group work Imagine you are leaving for a vacation. Decide where you will go, how long you will stay there, and what items you will take with you. Use the items in part A or your own ideas.

If we're going to go to China for a month, we'll need some warm clothes.

It depends when we go. If we go in the spring, we can take . . .

Destination: ________________　　Length of vacation: ________________

Clothing	Toiletries	Emergency items	Other items

E Group work Think of a time when you forgot to take something on a trip. What was it? What did you do?

10A Useful things

Activity 1 **A Pair work** Match the names of the inventions to these pictures.

1. **cell phone**
2. **food processor**
3. **microwave oven**
4. **camcorder**
5. **treadmill**
6. **mouse**
7. **fax machine**

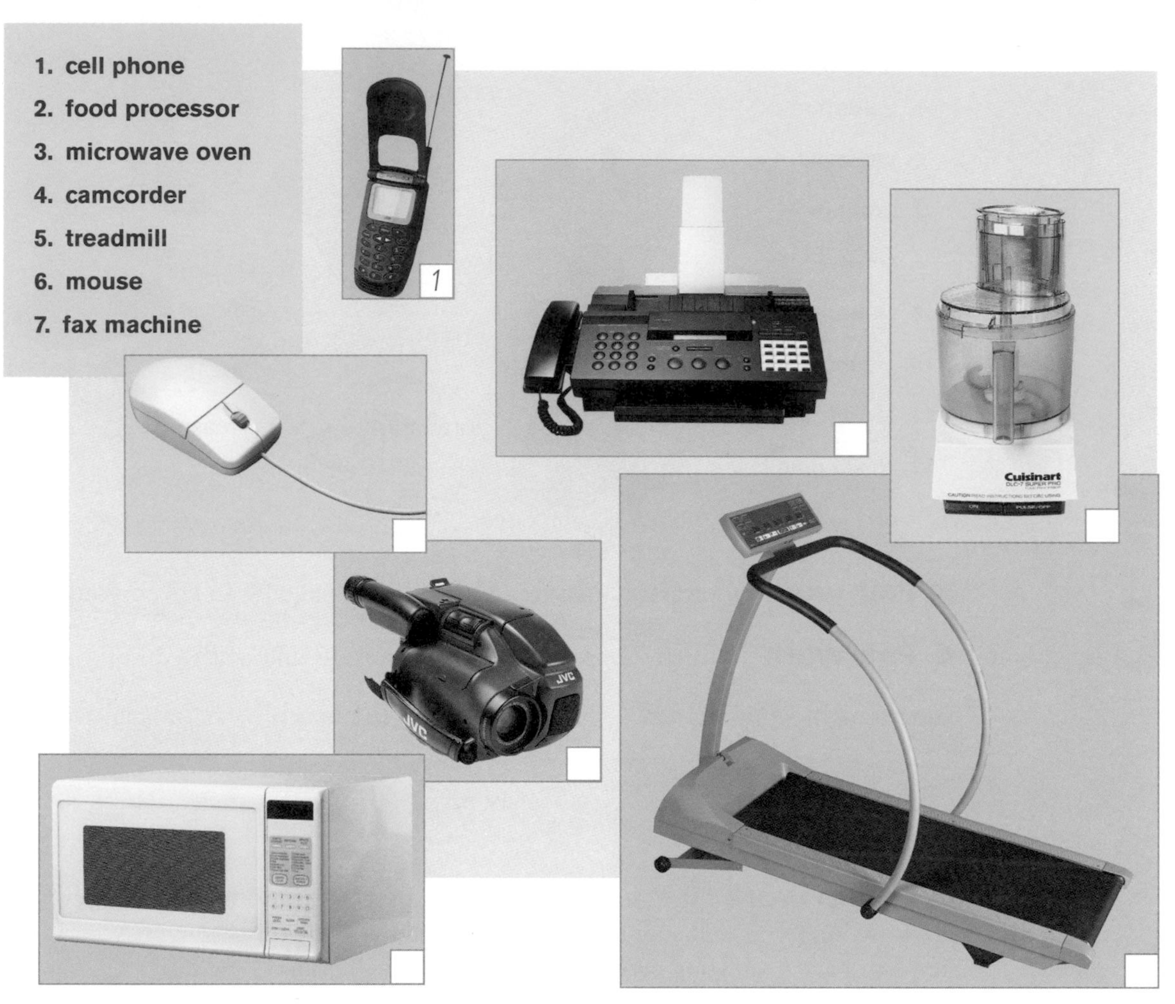

B Pair work Look at these definitions. Which of the things in part A does each one describe? Write the correct number.

..5... You use it to keep in good physical shape.
.... You use it to cook things very quickly.
.... You use it to point to items on a computer screen.
.... You use it to send a letter or picture to someone very quickly.
.... You use it to slice, chop, and blend things.
.... You use it to make calls when you're away from home.
.... You use it to help you remember vacations and special occasions.

C Join another pair Discuss these questions.

- Which items in part A do you use? How often?
- Which items do you hardly ever use?
- Which item do you think is the least useful?
- How would your life be different without the inventions?

I use my cell phone every day. I often need to . . .

Activity 2

A Pair work How necessary are these inventions to you? Write ✔✔ (very necessary), ✔ (necessary), or ✘ (not necessary) next to each item. Then compare with a partner.

...... answering machine	...... fax machine	...... remote control
...... cell phone	...... microwave oven	...... treadmill
...... computer	...... photocopier	...... TV
...... dishwasher	...... portable CD player	...... VCR

B Join another pair Compare your opinions. Give reasons.

I think an answering machine is very necessary. I'd miss important information without it.

C Group work Choose one of the inventions in part A. Tell the group how to use it.

To use a treadmill, you first set the speed. You start to walk . . .

Activity 3

A Listen Three people are shopping for these products. Check (✔) the features of each one.

1. CD player	☐ **a good price**	☐ **lightweight**
	☐ **a long battery life**	☐ **an anti-shock feature**
	☐ **includes FM radio**	☐ **a variety of colors**
2. camcorder	☐ **costs less than $500**	☐ **a well-known brand**
	☐ **a small size**	☐ **lightweight**
	☐ **a nice design**	☐ **a color viewfinder**
3. notebook computer	☐ **costs less than $1,000**	☐ **lightweight**
	☐ **a nice design and color**	☐ **a long battery life**
	☐ **includes software**	☐ **plays DVD movies**

B Pair work Compare your answers. Which of the items would you buy?

SELF-STUDY *see page 101*

10B Great ideas?

Activity 1 **A Pair work** Look at the photos. What do you think is special about each product?

Pencorder | Safe-T-Man | TV Remote Control Locator

I'm not sure, but maybe the Pencorder is used for . . .

B Listen You will hear part of a TV show. Complete the chart.

Product	Function	One important feature	Price
1. Pencorder			
2. Safe-T-Man			
3. TV Remote Control Locator			

C Pair work Compare your answers. Then discuss these questions.

- Which products sound useful to you? not very useful?
- What product do you think is the most original? Why?
- What have you bought in the past few months that you're extremely pleased with? Why?
- What have you bought recently that you're disappointed with? Why?

The Pencorder sounds useful because I can use it in class.

Activity 2 **A Read/listen** First read the articles, and try to guess the missing words. Then listen and check your answers.

Yoshiro Nakamatsu

Dr. Yoshiro Nakamatsu ________ the first floppy disk in 1950. Nakamatsu, an ________ at Tokyo University in Japan, holds 2,900 other patents, including one for ________ club designs. IBM, a computer company, bought the sales license for the disks. They ________ Nakamatsu's design and started selling floppy disks in 1970.

Mary Anderson

The windshield wiper was invented in 1903 by Mary Anderson, a woman from Alabama, U.S.A. While Anderson was riding a ________ during a trip to New York City, she noticed that the driver often had to get out to wipe ________ from the windshield. She quickly drew an idea for a ________ windshield wiper in her sketchbook. Later she tried to sell her ________ to a Canadian company, but the company decided that the invention wouldn't be ________. Anderson gave up on trying to sell her ________ and never made any money from it.

B Pair work Read the articles again. Then answer these questions.

1. Which inventor made no money from the invention?
2. Which inventor holds almost 3,000 patents?
3. Which inventor got his or her idea in the winter?
4. Which inventor made an agreement with IBM?

C Pair work Discuss these questions.

- Which invention in part A do you think was more significant? Why?
- What other everyday inventions do you think are especially significant?

I think the floppy disk was more significant because it changed the way we store information.

D Group work Have you ever had an idea for an invention? Tell your group about it.

E Group work Think of a gadget or an invention. Describe it without saying what it is. The rest of the group should guess what's being described.

This is something most people use every morning. It's used to . . .

F Communication task Work in groups of three. One of you should look at Task 9 on page 77, one at Task 24 on page 83, and one at Task 34 on page 87. You're going to talk about some recent inventions.

11A Threats to our environment

Activity 1 **A Pair work** Look at these photos. Which of these environmental problems do you have in your country?

air pollution
overcrowding
water pollution

There's air and water pollution, but not overcrowding.

What about in the cities?

B Pair work Which of these problems do you think will cause the most damage to the world? Why? Rank them from 1 (the most serious) to 6 (the least serious).

.... More and more people are living in cities.
.... Rivers, lakes, and oceans are becoming more polluted.
.... The air in our cities is becoming more polluted.
.... The greenhouse effect is causing the earth's temperature to rise.
.... The population of the world is growing too quickly.
.... Holes are developing in the earth's ozone layer, the part of the atmosphere that protects the earth from dangerous radiation.

I think water pollution will cause the most damage because it will kill fish and other wildlife.

C Join another pair Discuss these questions.

- How do you think the world will be different 10 years from now? 50 years from now?
- What environmental problems will cause the most damage to your country?
- Who do you think is responsible for these problems? Why?

The air will probably be more polluted.

Activity 2

A Read/listen First read the article, and try to guess the missing words. Then listen and check your answers.

Medicinal Plants

When settlers in the United States spread west in the 1800s, they thought nothing of cutting down forests and killing ________ to develop their country.

Today, developing countries are cutting down their forests because their people want a better life. But ________ say that this is a disaster. The rain ________ are home to half the world's species. Undiscovered rain-forest plants could be used as ________ drugs to treat diseases like AIDS and cancer. Two of today's most powerful anti-cancer medicines come from a single rain-forest ________. Many kinds of plants, which could be the sources of tomorrow's cures, are being destroyed at the rate of ______ to ______ every day.

Developing countries think that it is wrong for people who ________ their own forests long ago to tell them not to develop. They also feel that when a drug company discovers a ______ in their rain forest, the company should share its profits with them.

B Pair work Compare your answers. Then discuss these questions.

- Is the cutting down of forests a problem in your country?
- Do you think developing countries have the right to cut down their forests? Why or why not?
- Does the world have the right to tell individual countries what to do with their rain forests?

It's a big problem. Many animals now have less space to live in.

C Pair work What everyday things do you use that may come from a rain forest? Make a list.

D Join another pair Compare your lists. Which things are necessary? unnecessary?

11B Saving the environment

Activity 1 **A Work alone** How "green" are you? Give each item in the quiz a number from 1 to 5.

1 = always   2 = often   3 = sometimes   4 = hardly ever   5 = never

How GREEN are you?

Do you . . . ?

	1. avoid throwing things away if they can be reused, repaired, or recycled
	2. use recycled paper
	3. recycle paper, glass, and cans
	4. avoid products from nonrenewable sources
	5. avoid buying overpackaged products
	6. walk or use a bike when traveling short distances
	7. use public transportation when traveling long distances
	8. avoid using the air-conditioning in the summer
	9. make sure the heat isn't turned up too high in the winter
	10. use low-energy lightbulbs
	11. turn off the lights when you leave a room
	12. avoid using more water than you need

B Pair work Add up the numbers from the quiz above. Turn to page 90 to calculate your score. Who is more "green"?

C Join another pair Discuss these questions.

- Which item from the quiz do you think is the most important thing to do? the least important?
- What other "green" things do you do?
- Is recycling popular in your country? Is it required?

The most important thing to do is use recycled paper.

Do you think so? I think it's important to . . .

Activity 2 **A Listen** Five people are talking about recycling these items. Write down the item each person is talking about. Then write one way the item can be recycled.

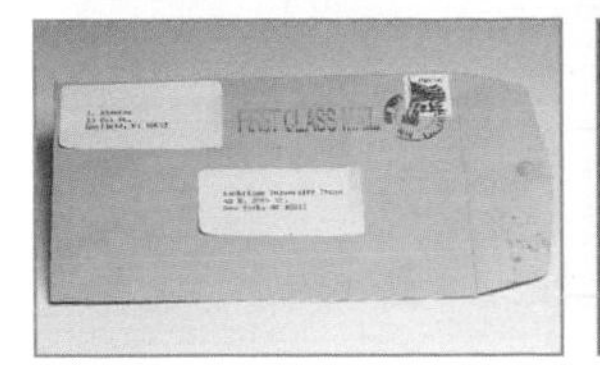
a used envelope

old reports

an empty container

a chipped cup

used aluminum foil

Item	One way to recycle
1. *old reports*	*use them for note paper*
2.	
3.	
4.	
5.	

B Pair work Compare your answers. Then discuss these questions.

- Which idea in part A seems the best to you? the worst?
- What are some other ways to recycle the things in part A?
- Can you think of ideas for recycling other things?

C Group work Look at the photos. Then discuss the questions below.

- What is happening in each photo?
- What benefits to the environment do you see in each photo?

The wind is creating energy. It's good because it's a clean form of energy.

D Communication task Work with a partner. One of you should look at Task 10 on page 77, and the other at Task 25 on page 83. You're going to talk about environmental problems and solutions.

SELF-STUDY *see page 102*

12A In the news

Activity 1 **A Pair work** Look at these news photos. What is happening? Describe each photo using the words in the box or your own words.

It looks like some buildings are on fire. There is a lot of smoke, and a police officer is calling . . .

B Join another pair What do you think each news story is about? What happened before and after each photo was taken?

I think some campers started the fire. I think they were cooking and . . .

C Listen You will hear part of a news broadcast. Match the news stories to the pictures in part A. Number the pictures from 1 to 4.

D Listen again Complete the summaries of the news stories.

1. Strong .... drove forest fire .... toward the city of Bellevue. Hundreds of .... had to leave their homes. The fire is now under ....

2. Mary Avona was .... from a boat by helicopter and taken to the .... She had an .... to remove her appendix. Doctors say it was a ....

3. A whale swam into the .... and was unable to return to the ocean. Over the weekend, sight-seers .... the whale. Divers were able to calm the whale down and .... it to the open ocean.

4. Stacy Baxter met her .... sister, Alicia Carson, for the first time. They were .... at birth and lived with two different families.

E Group work Compare your summaries. Which story had the happiest ending?

Activity 2

A Pair work Choose one of these photos. What do you think happened? Prepare a news summary.

B Join another pair Present your news summaries. Which pair has the most interesting summary?

Two women decided to have a contest. They wanted to see how long they could . . .

Activity 3

A Pair work What were the five most important news stories last year? Discuss and prepare a list.

B Join another pair Compare your lists. Try to agree on a single list.

We think . . . was the most important news story last year.

Really? Don't you think . . . was more important?

SELF-STUDY *see page 103*

12B Keep up to date!

Activity 1 **A Work alone** Complete the questionnaire.

the news & current events

1 How much time do you spend learning about the news every day?

.... less than 10 minutes .... 10–30 minutes .... more than 30 minutes

2 How do you learn about the news? Write O (Often), S (Sometimes), or N (Never).

.... radio	.... weekly newsmagazine
.... TV	.... Internet
.... daily newspaper	.... other ....

3 Which sections do you read in a newspaper? Which do you usually ignore?
Write R (Read) or I (Ignore).

.... world news	.... weather	.... sports
.... national news	.... arts	.... business news
.... local news	.... comics	.... other ....

B Group work Compare your answers. What do you have in common with your group? How are you different?

I often watch the news on TV.

I do, too. I never use the Internet.

C Communication task Work with a partner. Study the picture for only 10 seconds. One of you should then look at Task 11 on page 78, and the other at Task 26 on page 84. You're going to answer questions about the picture.

Activity 2 **A Read/listen** First read the news articles, and try to guess the missing words. Then listen and check your answers.

①

WALKMAN REVENGE

A ________ commuter in England was so angry at the ________ coming from a young man's Walkman that he took a pair of scissors from his ________ and cut through the headphone wire. His fellow ________ applauded.

②

TIME IS MONEY

A woman in Chicago was very ________ when her ex-husband remarried. While he and his new wife were on their ________, she broke into his apartment and ________ the "speaking clock" in London for the time. She left the phone off the hook and went home. The phone was off the hook until the ________ got back from vacation two weeks later. The phone ________ came to over $8,000.

③

Virtual Baby

For people who like ________ but don't have the time for a family, Quality Video of Minneapolis, Minnesota, U.S.A., has ________ "Video Baby." This 30-minute tape shows two babies doing what babies do, like crawl around the house, ________ with a rattle, take a bubble bath, and turn ________ into a complete mess. There's no narrator, so once the ________ is in the VCR, there's nothing to come between the viewer and the baby but the ________ button.

B Pair work Give a one-sentence summary of each story.

The first story is about someone who was so angry that . . .

C Group work Discuss these questions.

- What recent news story upset you most? amused you?
- Do you think it's important to keep up to date about the news? Why?
- Do you believe everything you hear on the news or read in the newspapers?

The recent story about . . . really upset me.

Review puzzles

Puzzle A

Use the clues to complete the puzzle with words from Unit 9.

Across

1. I took my toothpaste, but forgot to take my .... .
2. A place a lot of tourists don't go to can be .... .
3. Visit the .... of Modern Art if you go to New York.
4. Most parts of Alaska are .... areas.
5. Buy a .... and read about the places you're going to visit.
6. If you're going abroad, you need a .... .
7. I like vacationing in a place with a warm .... .
8. It's hot. Let's go to the .... and swim.
9. Why stay overnight there? Just take a day .... .
10. You need this at the beach.
11. We took the .... across the harbor.
12. Is it safe to swim in the .... ?
13. New York City is famous for its .... .
14. lots of trees
15. a sort of frozen river?
16. The Alps are a chain of .... .
17. Mt. Fuji is one.
18. Have you ever taken an .... vacation?

Down

19. What are the most interesting .... in your city?

19

1 *t o o t h b r u s h*

2

3

4

5

6

7

8

9

10

11

12

13

14

15

16

17

18

Puzzle B

1. Here are 6 scrambled words. Unscramble the letters to make words from Lesson 10A.

noninvite	i *n v e n t i (o) n*
usome	m (_) _ _ _
signed	d _ _ _ _ (_)
macroview	m _ _ (_) _ _ _ _ _
redramcoc	c _ (_) _ _ _ _ _ _ _
toperichpoo	p _ (_) _ _ (_) _ _ _ _ (_)

2. Here are 6 more scrambled words. Unscramble the letters to make words from Lesson 10B.

tagged	g *a d g (e) t*
afurete	f (_) _ _ _ _ _
antpet	p _ _ _ _ _
artistbee	b _ (_) _ _ _ _ _ _
sinewildhd	w _ _ _ (_) _ _ _ (_) _
justbadale	a _ _ _ _ (_) _ _ _ _

3. Now use the letters in the circles above to complete the sentence.

"How many _ _ _ _ _ _ _ _ _ _ _ _ _ _ _ do you have?"

Puzzle C

There are 20 words from Unit 11 in this word search puzzle. How many can you find? They all have something to do with NATURE and the ENVIRONMENT.

Puzzle D

Use the clues to solve the puzzle with words from Unit 12.

Across

2. International news is news from other parts of the .... .
4. Are you interested in the news and .... events?
6. .... news is news about your country.
8. I listen to the news on the .... in my car.
11. The firefighters managed to .... everyone from the building.
12. He looks at the .... forecast in the paper before deciding what to wear.
14. *Time* is the best-known American .... .
15. Which .... of the paper do you look at first?
16. I get .... when I hear about bad news.

Down

1. .... news is news about your city or region.
3. *The New York Times* is a .... newspaper.
5. a short version of the news
7. I read an interesting .... in the paper about whales.
9. The latest news is always available on the .... .
10. Don't .... everything you read in the newspaper!
13. He has no sense of humor. He never looks at the .... in the paper.

13A City life

Activity 1

A Pair work Look at these photos of city life. Describe each photo using the words in the box or your own words.

construction
grass
inconvenient
litter
noisy
park
time-consuming
traffic jam

B Listen Kevin lives in the country. Jeffrey lives in the city. They are both talking about the advantages of where they live. Take notes on what they say.

Advantages of city life	Advantages of country life
interesting, good jobs	*quieter*

C Pair work Compare your notes. Then discuss these questions.

- What are some other advantages of living in the city? in the country?
- Where would you prefer to live? Why?
- How would you describe the city or town where you live? What do you like and dislike about it?

One good thing about city life is the variety of restaurants.

SELF-STUDY *see page 104*

Activity 2 **A Pair work** Look at these profiles of San Francisco and New York City. Then answer the questions below.

	San Francisco	New York City
population	735,315	7,380,906
cost of home	$550,000	$820,000
unemployment rate	3.3%	8.1%
snowfall	0 centimeters per year	74 centimeters per year
rainfall	53 centimeters per year	102 centimeters per year
crimes committed per 100,000 people	7,595	5,212

1 centimeter = .39 inches

Which city would you recommend to someone who . . . ?

is desperate to find a job
wants to buy a first home
is concerned about crime
likes winter sports
enjoys being around a lot of people
hates wet weather

If someone is desperate to find a job, I would recommend San Francisco.

B Pair work Discuss these questions.

- What's the largest city you've ever been to? What was it like there?
- What's your favorite city to visit? Why?
- If you could choose a city to live in, which would it be? Why?

The largest city I've been to is Taipei. It was crowded but very exciting.

C Join another pair Where would you tell people to live in your country if they wanted a city with these things?

good shopping
clean air
interesting restaurants
beautiful old buildings
a low crime rate
the best university
easy access to wilderness
good employment opportunities
lots of cultural events

If they want good shopping, they should live in . . .

D Communication task Work with a partner. One of you should look at Task 12 on page 78, and the other at Task 27 on page 84. You're going to look at some information about different cities around the world.

13B Safety and crime

Activity 1

A Work alone Fill out this questionnaire. Which of these things do you do to protect yourself against crime? Which of these things do you avoid doing? Check (✔) the things you do.

Do you . . . ?	Do you avoid . . . ?
☐ carry a flashlight or a personal alarm	☐ wearing jewelry on the street
☐ keep car doors locked at traffic lights	☐ making eye contact with strangers
☐ carry only a small amount of cash	☐ taking public transportation late at night
☐ carry only one credit card	☐ talking to strangers
☐ walk only on well-lit streets	☐ going out alone at night

B Pair work Compare your answers. Do you do the same things to protect yourself against crime? How are you different?

We both avoid making eye contact with strangers.

Neither of us carries a flashlight.

Activity 2

A Listen 🎧 Three people are talking about crime and safety where they live. Who is talking? Look at the chart, and check (✔) the correct column.

Who . . . ?	*Larry*	*Anne*	*Paul*
stands near other people while waiting for the subway			
has locks on the windows of his/her apartment			
avoids making eye contact with people on the street			
has his/her apartment keys ready			
doesn't walk alone late at night			
doesn't let strangers into his/her apartment building			
rides in the subway car with the conductor late at night			
always looks like he/she knows where he/she's going			
tells his/her roommate where he/she's going			

B Pair work Compare your answers. Then discuss these questions.

- Do you do any of the things that the people in part A mentioned? Which ones?
- What other things do you do to stay safe?

I don't walk alone at night or let strangers into my building.

Activity 3 **A Pair work** Look at the graph. Then discuss the questions below.

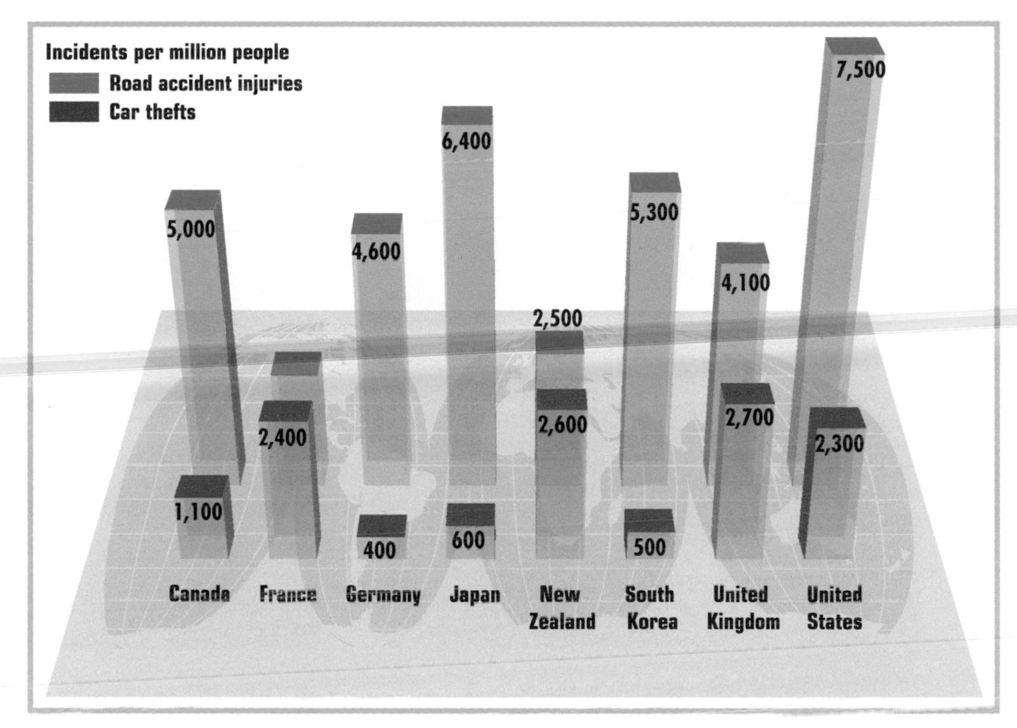

- Which country is the safest?
- How safe is your country? If it's not in the graph, how do you think it compares to the countries listed above?
- Do you worry about crime where you live? when you travel to another city or country?

When it comes to road accidents, . . . is the safest.

B Work alone Read each situation. Then number the list from 1 (the most serious) to 7 (the least serious).

.... A couple stole food because they were hungry and had no money.
.... A group of people started fighting with each other. No one else was involved.
.... A person rode the subway without paying.
.... Some teenagers painted graffiti on the wall of a building.
.... A person threw away an empty coffee cup on the sidewalk.
.... An office worker took home pens and stationery for personal use.
.... A politician received a lot of money from a businessperson.

C Group work Compare your evaluations. Do you think all the situations in part B are crimes? Why or why not?

I don't think riding the subway without paying is a crime.

Of course it's a crime! It's a form of stealing.

14A Yes, but is it art?

Activity 1 **A Pair work** Look at these works of art. What are your reactions to each one? Use the words in the box or your own words to talk about each picture.

painting/sculpture
abstract/figurative
modern/traditional
realistic/nonrealistic/surrealistic
portrait/still life/landscape

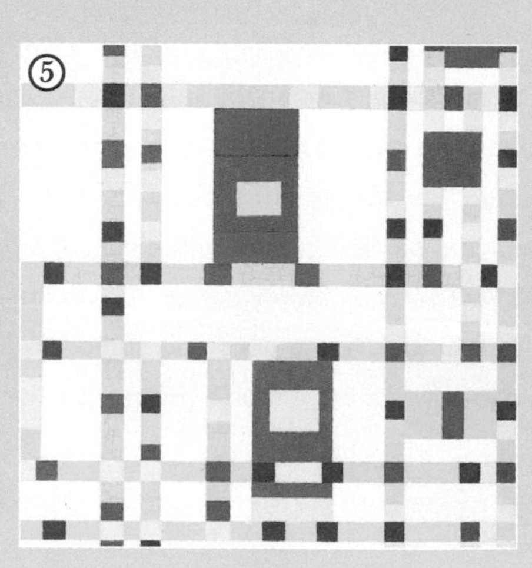

I really like the abstract painting. I love the bright colors.

Really? I'm not sure I like abstract art.

B Join another pair Discuss these questions.

- Which work of art in part A do you like the most? Why?
- What kind of art do you like? Do you prefer painting or sculpture? abstract art or realistic art? modern art or traditional art?
- Do you have a favorite artist? Who is it? Why do you like his or her art?

I like the picture of the flower the most. I love still-life paintings.

C Group work Try to match these artists to their art in part A. Then turn to page 90 to check your answers.

...4... **Xu Beihong** (1895–1953) known for traditional paintings of horses	.... **Piet Mondrian** (1872–1944) known for abstract paintings that use horizontal and vertical blocks of bright colors
.... **Fernando Botero** (1932–) known for figurative paintings and sculptures of heavy, muscular people	.... **Georgia O'Keeffe** (1887–1986) known for realistic still-life paintings of flowers
.... **Frida Kahlo** (1907–1954) known for surrealistic self-portraits	.... **Nicolas Poussin** (1594–1665) known for realistic landscapes

Activity 2 **A Pair work** What makes something a "work of art"? Check (✔) the reasons.

- ☐ unique
- ☐ expensive to produce
- ☐ extremely beautiful
- ☐ loved by everyone
- ☐ thought-provoking
- ☐ created by a human

B Group work Look at these things. Are they art? Compare your opinions.

C Group work Can these things ever be "works of art"? In what circumstances?

a building   a novel   a song   clothing   a meal

A meal could never be art.

It depends on how you define "art."

D Communication task Work in pairs. Both of you should look at Task 37 on page 88. You're going to talk about paintings.

14B I really enjoyed it!

Activity 1

A Listen You will hear a tune recorded in five different musical styles. As you listen, give each example a grade.

1. _____
2. _____
3. _____
4. _____
5. _____

A = This is great! I love this kind of music.
B = This is good music.
C = This music is OK, but it's not my favorite.
D = I don't like this kind of music very much.
F = I hate this kind of music.

B Listen again Match each piece of music to the description.

1. _____	a. country and western
2. _____	b. jazz
3. _____	c. classical
4. _____	d. easy listening
5. _____	e. heavy metal

C Pair work Compare your answers. What kinds of music do you enjoy that you did not hear in the recording?

D Pair work Do you know the names of these musical instruments? Write the names under the pictures.

1. ______________ 2. ______________ 3. ______________ 4. ______________

5. ______________ 6. ______________ 7. ______________ 8. ______________

E Join another pair Turn to page 90 to check your answers. Then discuss these questions.

- Can you play a musical instrument? What instrument would you like to be able to play?
- What's your favorite kind of music? Why do you like it?
- Who's your favorite male singer? female singer? band?
- What's your favorite song?

I can play the violin a little. I'd like to be able to play the flute.

Activity 2 **A Read/listen** First read the movie review, and try to guess the missing words. Then listen and check your answers.

Meet the Applegates

The Applegates seem like many other American ________. Father Dick is a security guard at a power plant. Mother Jane is a homemaker. ________ Sally and Johnny are great kids. But what no one knows is that the Applegates are really ________! They come from the Amazon rain ________ and have disguised themselves as humans so that they can start a campaign to stop people from ________ their home.

While they're ________ their campaign, the Applegates try to make friends and act like a normal family (which isn't easy since they only eat ________ and liquid sugar!). But they soon have ________. Jane starts charging too much on her new ________ cards, and both Johnny and Sally get into trouble. Dick has trouble with his ________. But thankfully Aunt Bea Applegate arrives to ________ the day!

Packed with ________ special effects, witty observations, and plenty of ________, *Meet the Applegates* is a ________ film with an environmental theme.

B Pair work Compare your answers. Would you like to see the film? Why or why not?

C Group work Discuss these questions.

- Which recent movie would you recommend? Tell your group the story without giving away the ending.
- Who's your favorite movie director? What is his or her best movie?
- Who are your two favorite female and two favorite male movie stars? Why do you like them? What are their best movies?

This movie is about two people who fall in love. At first, they're really happy, but . . .

SELF-STUDY *see page 105*

15A Times have changed . . .

Activity 1 **A Pair work** These photos are of the same person's desk 15 years ago and today. How old do you think this person was 15 years ago?

B Join another pair Discuss these questions.

- Do you think this person is male or female? Why?
- What was this person like 15 years ago? What is he or she like now?
- How has your room or home changed in the last 15 years?

I think this person is . . . because on the desk there's . . .

Activity 2 **A Listen** Three people are talking about what life was like when they were 12 years old. Who is talking? Look at the chart, and check (✔) the correct column.

Who . . . ?	*Phil*	*Wanda*	*Tom*
slept in the same room as his/her brother and sisters			
went on his/her first date			
loved playing games			
liked being treated as a friend by his/her father			
loved comic books			
loved making up stories			
hid in the museum with his/her girlfriend			
loved sports			
was spoiled because he/she was the youngest			

B Listen Now Phil, Wanda, and Tom are answering this question: "How was your life different then from the way it is now?" Take notes on their answers.

Phil	*fewer responsibilities then*
Wanda	
Tom	

C Pair work Compare your answers. Then discuss these questions.

- What do you remember most about being 12 years old?
- What did you like best about being 12?
- How is your life different now?
- Would you like to be 12 again? Why or why not?

What I remember most about being 12 was when I . . .

D Group work What was the best year of your life? Why?

The best year of my life was definitely 1998. That was the year I . . .

E Communication task Work in groups of four. Two of you should look at Task 13 on page 79, and the other two at Task 28 on page 85. You're going to tell a story about something that happened to you in the past.

SELF-STUDY *see page 106*

15B A sense of history

Activity 1 **Pair work** How good are you at history? Try to match these buildings to the dates they were completed on the time line. Then turn to page 90 to check your answers.

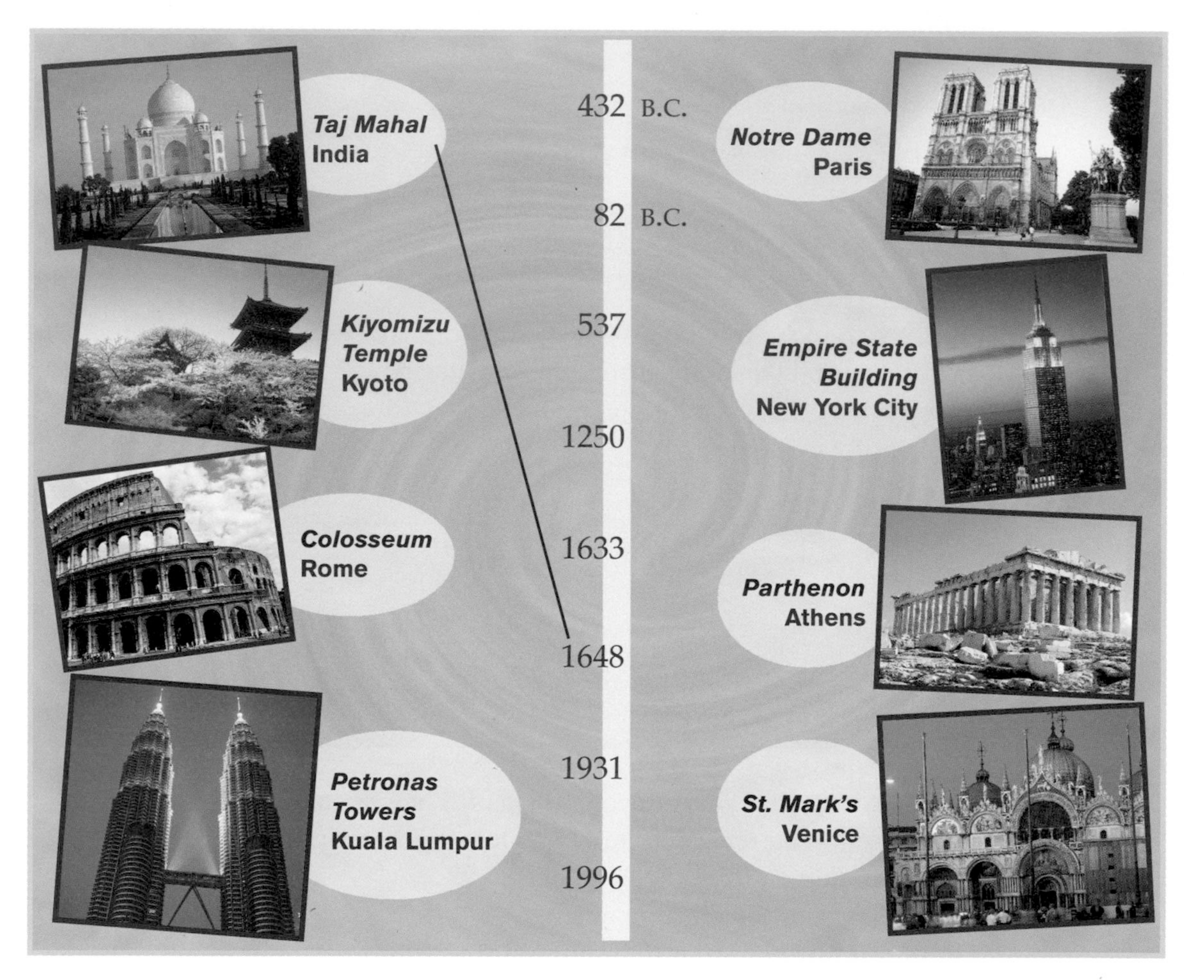

I think the Parthenon was completed in 537.

Are you sure? I think it's older.

Activity 2 **A Pair work** Make a list of the important historic sites in your own country. Then discuss these questions.

- Which of the places have you visited? What do you remember best about them?
- Are there any places you haven't visited that you would like to visit?
- If a visitor to your country had time to see only one thing, what should it be?

B Work alone Imagine that you're going to talk to a foreign tourist about your country. Write down the answers to these questions.

- Which historic buildings or places should he or she visit?
- What can you tell the tourist about the history of your country?

C Pair work Role-play a conversation between yourself and a foreign tourist. Talk about the history of your country and the places a tourist can visit.

To understand our history, you need to visit Mt. Fuji.

Why is a mountain important?

Activity 3

A Pair work What are the five most important events that happened in your country's history? Make a list.

B Join another pair Compare your lists and draw a time line with all the events. Which event do you think was the most significant? Why?

Activity 4

A Read/listen First read the descriptions, and try to guess the missing words. Then listen and check your answers.

Teotihuacán

Two thousand years ago, Teotihuacán, located north of Mexico City, was the largest ________ in the Americas, the capital of a powerful state with 100,000 inhabitants. It began to decline after 600 A.D. and was eventually abandoned and burned. When the Aztecs discovered the ________ years later, they believed the city had been ________ by gods. Visitors can ________ along the Avenue of the Dead to the enormous Temple of the Sun, from which there is a ________ of the ruined city. Every evening a sound and light show tells the story of the ________ city and its people.

Stonehenge

Scientists estimate that Stonehenge, a ________ in Wiltshire, England, dates from 2000 B.C., but nobody knows why it was built. It consists of a circle of 30 upright stone pillars connected with flat ________ laid across the top. Within the circle are five big stones in a horseshoe pattern and one pillar that faces the ________. Because of this, some people think Stonehenge was an ancient observatory. Others, however, believe it was a temple and ________ ground. Although ________ can't touch the stones, they can view them from behind a fence.

B Pair work Compare your answers. Then discuss these questions.

- Which place in part A would you rather visit? Why?
- Do you have similar places in your country? Where?

I'd rather visit Stonehenge. It sounds so mysterious.

16A What a scream!

Activity 1 **A Pair work** Look at these scenes from movies. Which scene looks the funniest? Why?

B Pair work Discuss these questions.

- What's the funniest movie you've ever seen?
- What's the funniest movie you've seen recently? What was your favorite funny scene?

The funniest movie I've ever seen is . . .

C Pair work Make a list of the top three funniest movies.

D Join another pair Compare your lists. Try to agree on a new top-three list.

Activity 2 **A Pair work** Circle the words below that you don't know, and ask your partner to explain them. Use a dictionary to look up any that neither of you knows. Then add the words to the chart.

cartoonist	comedian	giggle	satire
chuckle	comical	hilarious	slapstick
clown	farce	humorous	snicker

Types of humor	Funny people	Words for "funny"	Words for "laugh"
	cartoonist		

B Pair work Use the words above to talk about the scenes in Activity 1A.

Activity 3 **A Class activity** Do you recognize any of these people? What do you know about them? Who do you think is the funniest?

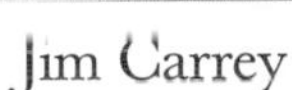

Jim Carrey | Whoopi Goldberg | Mike Myers | Mr. Bean

Mr. Bean doesn't speak, but he's hilarious because he . . .

B Pair work Discuss these questions.

- Who's the funniest person in your own country? How would you describe his or her style of humor to a foreign visitor?
- Are there a lot of female comedians in your country? Why or why not?
- Do you watch comedy shows on TV? If so, which are your favorites and what do you like about them? If not, why not?
- What's the most popular comedy show in your country? Why is it so popular?

. . . is really funny. She does a lot of slapstick and . . .

C Communication task Work in groups of three. One of you should look at Task 14 on page 79, one at Task 29 on page 85, and one at Task 36 on page 88. You're going to tell some jokes to your partners.

16B A sense of humor

Activity 1

A Pair work Look at these cartoons, and number them from 1 (the funniest) to 4 (the least funny).

"You know what we need? We need some of those colored golf balls."

"On the Internet, nobody knows you're a dog."

"We just haven't been flapping them hard enough."

"Would you like to hear some music while you hold?"

B Join another pair Compare your reactions to the cartoons. Why is each cartoon funny or not funny?

The first cartoon is hilarious. I love that kind of humor.

I don't get it.

C Group work Discuss these questions.

- Do you read the cartoons in the newspaper? If so, what's your favorite?
- Do you like to tell jokes? Why or why not?
- Think of the last time you had a good laugh. What was it about?

I always read the cartoons. My favorite is . . .

Activity 2 **A Listen** You will hear three stories. Before the end of each story, you will hear a bell. Try to guess the ending. Then listen to the rest of the story to check your guess.

B Listen again Put the pictures in each story in order from 1 to 4.

C Communication task Work in groups of three. One of you should look at Task 15 on page 79, one at Task 30 on page 85, and one at Task 35 on page 87. You're going to make up stories about some pictures.

SELF-STUDY *see page 107*

Review puzzles

Puzzle A

Use the clues to complete the puzzle with words from Unit 13.

Across

1. People in a city have good .... opportunities.
2. But people in the .... may have a better quality of life.
3. You often see this on walls in a city.
4. .... may just be friends you just haven't met yet!
5. Cities have plenty of cultural .... .
6. a popular pastime in the city
7. Do you avoid wearing .... on the street?
8. Many cities in Europe are full of beautiful old .... .
9. The .... of New York City is over 7 million.
10. It's important for a city to have .... public transportation.
11. Road .... are less serious if cars go slower.
12. People who .... crimes should be punished.
13. If you live in a city, you probably live in an .... .
14. a quick way to get around a big city

Down

15. I can't decide whether London or Hong Kong is ....

15

1 *e m p l o y m e n t*

2

3

4

5

6

7

8

9

10

11

12

13

14

Puzzle B

1. Here are 6 scrambled words. Unscramble the letters to make words from Lesson 14A.

riotpart	p *o r t (r) a i t*
tills file	s _ _ _ _ _ _ _ _ _
radiant toil	t _ _ (_) _ _ _ _ _ _ _ _
ladpances	l _ _ _ _ _ _ _ (_)
guitarfive	f _ _ _ _ _ _ _ _ _
cupresult	s _ _ _ _ _ _ _ _

2. Here are 6 more scrambled words. Unscramble the letters to make words from Lesson 14B.

aliasclcs	c *l a s s i c a l*
menintrust	i _ _ _ _ _ (_) _ _ _
viewer	r _ _ _ _ _
anoxhopes	s _ _ _ _ _ _ _ _
ivome rats	m (_) _ _ _ _ _ _ _
nivilo	v _ _ _ _ (_)

3. Now use the letters in the circles above to complete the sentence.

"I'm not crazy about _ _ _ _ _ _ art."

Puzzle C

There are 20 words from Unit 15 in this word search puzzle. How many can you find? They all have something to do with the PAST.

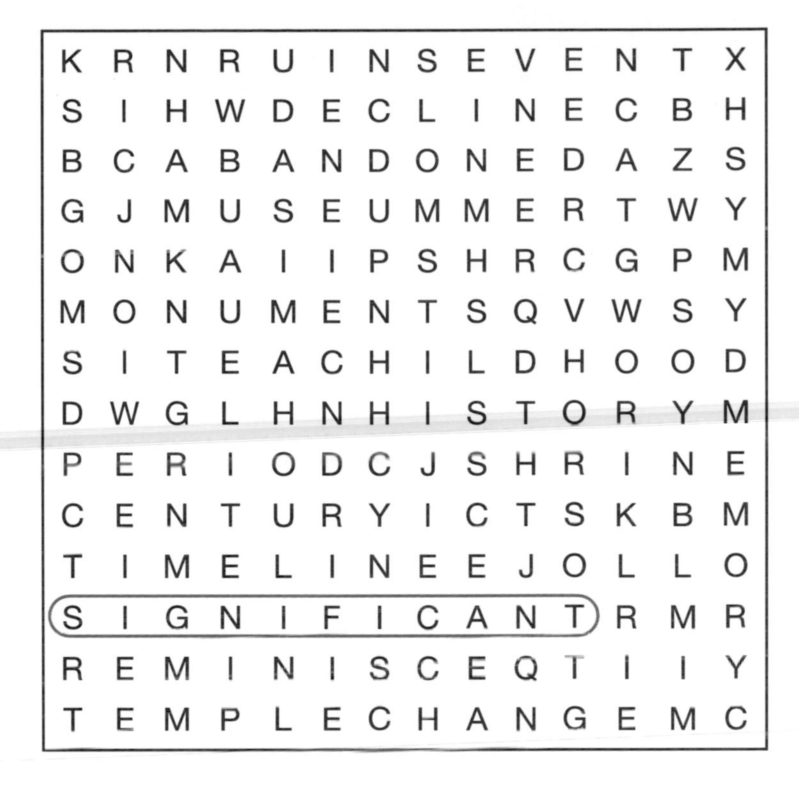

Puzzle D

Use the clues to solve the puzzle with words from Unit 16.

Across

1. Not everyone has the same .... of humor.
4. Is that movie supposed to be a .... ? I never laughed once.
6. Bart Simpson is my favorite .... character.
7. a quiet laugh about something ridiculous or silly
11. very, very funny
12. I'm hopeless at .... funny stories.
13. Do you know a .... in English?
14. a childish laugh about something silly
15. We all thought the joke was funny, but he didn't .... it.
16. a humorous way of criticizing people

Down

2. What was your favorite funny .... in the movie?
3. Falling over or being hit is common in this comedy style.
4. a funny person in a circus
5. ha ha!
8. Try to guess the .... of the story.
9. a funny play full of unlikely situations
10. What is the .... movie you've ever seen?

Communication tasks

Task 1 Ask your partner the questions in the survey below, and check (✔) the answers. Use the words in the box on the left to make statements about your partner's personality. Then your partner will ask you questions.

active/ relaxed

casual/ formal

shy/ outgoing

organized/ disorganized

neat/ messy

1. When you take a walk, do you usually walk . . . ?
   - ☐ fast
   - ☐ average speed
   - ☐ slow
2. When you go to a party, do you usually wear . . . ?
   - ☐ casual clothes like jeans and a T-shirt
   - ☐ more formal clothing
3. In your free time, do you prefer to . . . ?
   - ☐ read a book at home
   - ☐ go dancing with friends
4. Do you do your household chores in a systematic way?
   - ☐ yes
   - ☐ no
5. What does your bedroom look like?
   - ☐ The bed is unmade. Clothes are lying on the floor.
   - ☐ The bed is made. Clothes are in the dresser or closet.

I think you're an active person because you usually walk fast.

Task 2 Walk around the classroom, and find one person who answers YES to each question. Then ask an additional question to get more information. Write the person's name and the additional information. Try to get a different student's name for each question.

Do you live in an apartment, Anna?

Yes, I do.

Who . . . ?	Name	Additional information
1. lives in an apartment		
2. has a pet		
3. wants to go to graduate school		
4. knows how to say "Good morning" in three languages		

When you finish, rejoin your group. Tell them what you learned about your classmates.

Anna lives in an apartment. Her apartment is located . . .

Task 3 You are going to play the role of a waiter/waitress in a restaurant. The other people in your group will be customers. Give them the menu you wrote, and answer any questions. Then take their order.

Do you have any questions before I take your order?

Task 4 You have just moved to a new town and want to make some friends. Look at the pictures of these people, and listen to your partner tell you about them. Then choose one person you would like to be friends with. Explain your choice.

Scott Simmons

Debbie Malnick

Peter Ito

Now imagine that your partner has just moved to your town. Describe the three people below. Your partner will choose one person to be friends with. Ask your partner about his or her choice.

Pam Sawyer
age: 23
occupation: musician
hobbies: ballroom dancing, tennis, going to movies
motto: Take time to stop and smell the flowers.

Carlos Garcia
age: 25
occupation: teacher
hobbies: visiting museums, playing the violin, swimming
motto: If at first you don't succeed, try, try again.

Penny Lee
age: 34
occupation: designer
hobbies: hang gliding, bungee jumping, waterskiing
motto: There's an exception to every rule.

Pam Sawyer is 23 years old. She's a musician who likes . . .

Task 5 Read the descriptions of the two jobs, and then close your book. Describe the jobs to your group without mentioning the job titles. Ask your group to guess which jobs you're talking about.

This person works on a movie set when animals are being used in a movie. It is this person's job to teach animals how to perform in front of the camera. They work with all kinds of animals. They teach dogs to sit, bears to dance, and dolphins to jump.
(animal trainer)

This person sets up and moves the equipment on a movie set and also helps with the lights and cameras. This person is in charge of renting any equipment that is needed on the movie set. He or she must know what all of the equipment is used for.
(grip)

Task 6 Ask your partner about these activities, and write his or her answers below. Then answer your partner's questions.

Have you ever been bungee jumping? ....

If so, what was it like? ....

If not, would you like to try it? Why or why not? ....

....

....

Have you ever been waterskiing? ....

If so, what was it like? ....

If not, would you like to try it? Why or why not? ....

....

....

Task 7 Take turns playing these word games. Read the rules and explain them to your group.

"What's in Johnny's pocket?"
The first player begins like this: There's an *apple* in Johnny's pocket.
The second player continues: There's an *apple* and a *bear* in his pocket.
The third player continues: There's an *apple,* a *bear,* and a *cookie* in Johnny's pocket.

Continue through the alphabet until someone can't remember or think of a word.

Task 8 Look at these vacation snapshots. Decide what you think happened next, and describe it to your partner.

A man and a woman were fishing. The man was trying to bring in a fish, but . . .

Listen to your partner's descriptions. What did the vacations have in common?

Task 9 Look at these photos. Work together and try to guess what the products do. How do you think they work?

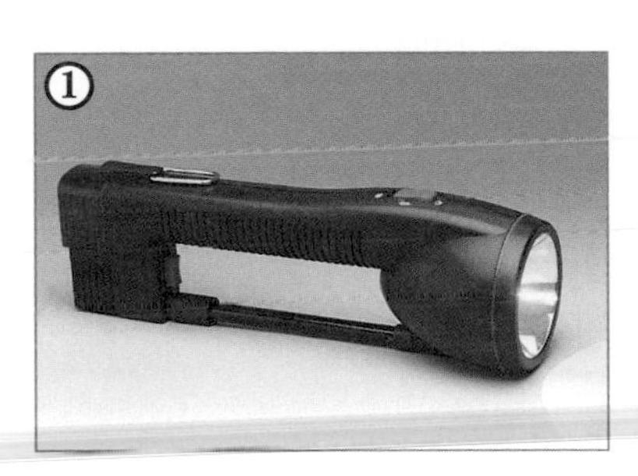

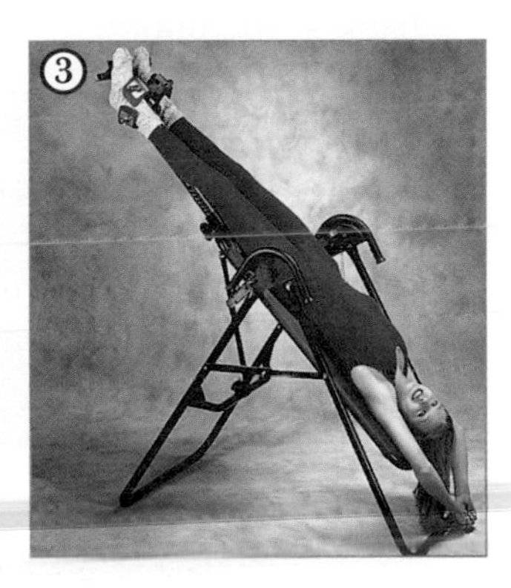

Each person in your group has a description of one of the items above. Take turns asking and answering questions about the products. Find out as much information as you can.

Picture One

Litemate

It's a flashlight, an emergency flasher, and a lighter!

LITEMATE combines three useful lights in one unit. You can use it at home, in your car, or when you're camping. LITEMATE is perfect for emergencies. On one end of LITEMATE, there's a flashlight. On the other end, there's a red emergency light that flashes. At the bottom, there's a long lighter that comes apart from the rest of the unit. It's perfect for lighting candles or starting a campfire. Uses four batteries.

$29.95

What is it used for?

Task 10 What environmental problems do the photos show? Describe the problems to your partner. Your partner will suggest some solutions.

littering

traffic jams

The first photo shows a lot of ugly litter, such as bottles, cans, and . . .

Task 11 Are you a reliable witness? Write the answers to the questions about the photo on page 52. Then ask your partner the questions, and write the answers. Do *not* look back at the photo.

	You	Your partner
1. How many men are in the room?	....	....
2. How many people are sitting down?	....	....
3. What color shirt is the man on the right wearing?	....	....
4. What is the woman near the window wearing?	....	....
5. Which of the people is wearing glasses?	....	....

Compare your answers. Then look back at the photo to check your answers.

Task 12 You want to visit one of the cities pictured below, but need to find out more information about each one before making a choice.

New Orleans, Louisiana, U.S.A.

Rio de Janeiro, Brazil

Ask your partner questions about:

the weather   popular foods   popular tourist sights

What's the weather like in New Orleans?

After you find out about the cities, choose the one you would most like to visit. Then answer your partner's questions about the cities below. Ask your partner to choose a city to visit and to explain his or her choice.

SEOUL, SOUTH KOREA
Average temperature January –1°C/30°F   June 27°C/81°F
Food specialties *Bulgogi*: beef marinated with soy sauce and other spices *Kimchi*: a spicy dish made of cabbage
Tourist attractions *Secret Garden*: part of a royal palace – famous for its beautiful scenery *Namdaemun Market*: a great place to shop for bargains *Mt. Puk'ansan*: a national park with Buddhist temples and hiking paths

VENICE, ITALY
Average temperature January 4°C/40°F   June 27°C/81°F
Food specialties *Fegato alla Veneziana*: calf's liver served on a bed of onions *Polenta*: grilled cornmeal served with sauce
Tourist attractions *Basilica di San Marco*: a cathedral with beautiful artwork, marble, and carvings *Rialto Quarter*: the oldest and busiest part of the city – a great place to shop *Lagoon Islands*: once the home of fishermen and hunters – now attract many tourists

Task 13 Imagine that the events below happened to both of you a long time ago. Using the pictures, talk about what happened. Add as many additional details as possible.

I'll never forget the time we went on a bicycling trip. Do you remember that?

How could I forget? I'll never forget the first day. It was so easy until . . .

Join another pair. Tell them what happened.

Task 14 Read these jokes and make sure you understand them. Then take turns telling them.

Doctor: You need glasses.
Woman: But I'm already wearing glasses.
Doctor: In that case, *I* need glasses.

Man: What's the secret to a long, happy marriage?
Woman: Well, my husband and I go out for a fancy dinner every week.
Man: That's wonderful! Where do you go?
Woman: I like Italian – I don't know where my husband goes.

Do you know any jokes? Tell one to your group.

Task 15 Think of a funny story to explain the photo below. Answer these questions.

- Who is the person in the photo?
- How did he end up in that situation?
- What's going to happen next?

Tell your story to your group.

Task 16

First answer your partner's questions. Then ask your partner the questions in the survey below, and check (✔) the answers. Use the words in the box on the left to make statements about your partner's personality.

active/ relaxed casual/ formal shy/ outgoing organized/ disorganized neat/ messy	1. In your free time, do you prefer to . . . ? ☐ play sports ☐ watch movies 2. What kind of party do you prefer? ☐ loud and crowded with music and dancing ☐ small and quiet with intimate conversation 3. How often do you talk to friends on the telephone? ☐ all the time ☐ fairly often ☐ not very often 4. When you shop, do you usually . . . ? ☐ make a list of what you need before you go out ☐ buy whatever looks good 5. When you use a textbook to study English, do you . . . ? ☐ write words and answers anywhere on the page ☐ write carefully on the lines provided

I think you're a relaxed person beacuse you prefer to watch movies.

Task 17

Walk around the classroom, and find one person who answers YES to each question. Then ask an additional question to get more information. Write the person's name and the additional information. Try to get a different student's name for each question.

Do you have an older sister, Mark?

Yes, I do.

Who . . . ?	Name	Additional information
1. has an older sister		
2. likes to cook		
3. belongs to a club		
4. knows how to sing a song in English		

When you finish, rejoin your group. Tell them what you learned about your classmates.

Mark has an older sister. Her name is . . .

Task 18 You are going to play the role of customers in a restaurant. The other person in your group will be the waiter/waitress. Look at the menu, and ask your server questions about the items. Then decide what to order.

> *We're not sure what this dish is. Can you explain it for us?*

Task 19 Imagine that your partner has just moved to your town and wants to make some friends. Describe the three people below. Your partner will choose one person to be friends with. Ask your partner about his or her choice.

Scott Simmons	Debbie Malnick	Peter Ito
age: 32 **occupation**: lawyer **hobbies**: reading, going to concerts, cooking **motto:** Actions speak louder than words.	**age**: 26 **occupation**: student **hobbies**: painting, dancing, in-line skating **motto:** Look before you leap.	**age**: 26 **occupation**: actor **hobbies**: sailing, rock climbing, traveling **motto:** Never walk when you can run.

> *Scott Simmons is 32 years old. He's a lawyer who likes . . .*

Now you have just moved to a new town and want to make some friends. Look at the pictures of these people, and listen to your partner tell you about them. Then choose one person you would like to be friends with. Explain your choice.

Pam Sawyer

Carlos Garcia

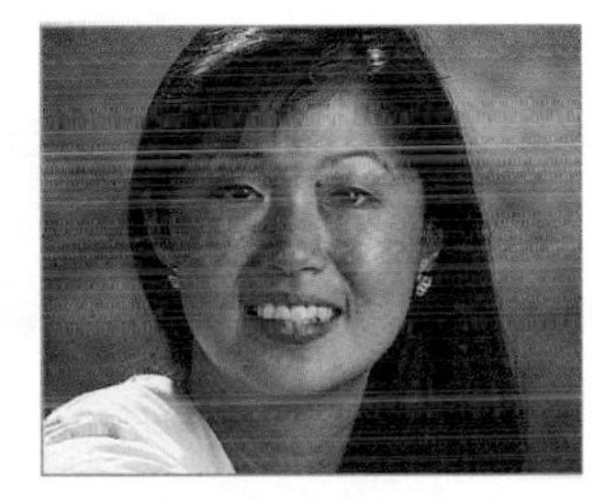
Penny Lee

Task 20 Read the descriptions of the two jobs, and then close your book. Describe the jobs to your group without mentioning the job titles. Ask your group to guess which jobs you're talking about.

This person looks through the lens of a camera and actually films the movie. He or she moves the camera to keep the actors in the movie scene. This person often sits above the actors in a seat attached to the camera to film a scene.
(cameraperson)

This person is always on the movie set. Sometimes he or she applies makeup, like lipstick, to bring out an actor's natural color under the lights on the set. Other times this person has to turn the actor into a different character, such as a monster or a clown.
(makeup artist)

Task 21 First answer your partner's questions. Then ask your partner about these activities, and write his or her answers below.

Have you ever been in a hot-air balloon? ....

If so, what was it like? ....

If not, would you like to try it? Why or why not? ....

....

....

Have you ever done in-line skating? ....

If so, what was it like? ....

If not, would you like to try it? Why or why not? ....

....

....

Task 22 Take turns playing these word games. Read the rules and explain them to your group.

Twenty questions

Think of a famous person. Tell the others in your group to ask *yes/no* questions about the person. Answer the questions, but remember only to answer by saying "yes" or "no."

The others can try to guess the person at any time.

Play until someone guesses correctly, or until they have asked twenty questions.

Task 23 Look at these vacation snapshots. Decide what you think happened next, and describe it to your partner.

A man and a woman were going scuba diving. The weather was becoming . . .

Listen to your partner's descriptions. What did the vacations have in common?

Task 24 Look at these photos. Work together and try to guess what the products do. How do you think they work?

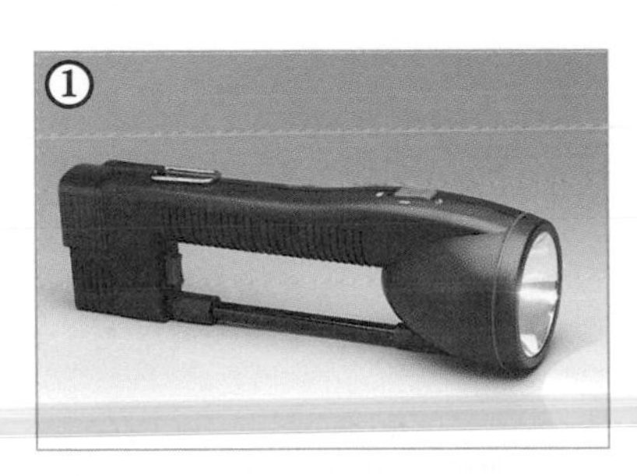

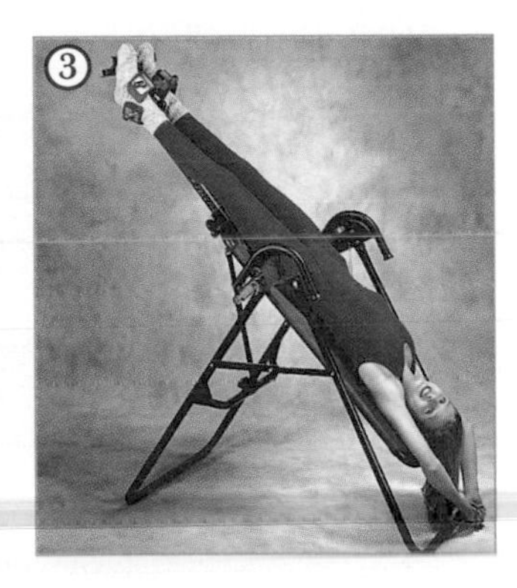

Each person in your group has a description of one of the items above. Take turns asking and answering questions about the products. Find out as much information as you can.

Picture Two

Sparkling Sip™ Straw

You'll have cleaner drinking water instantly!

The portable Sparkling Sip™ straw can go with you anywhere. It removes chlorine, and bad tastes and smells from drinking water. The Sparkling Sip™ straw uses two filters to clean your drinking water.

One filter removes up to 95% of the chlorine present in drinking water. The other filter removes bad tastes and smells. Includes replacement filters and a carrying case.

$12.95

What is it used for?

Task 25 Your partner is going to describe some environmental problems to you. Look at the photos below, and suggest some solutions to the problems.

recycling

using public transportation

One possible solution to the problem is recycling. Also, it's useful to . . .

Task 26

Are you a reliable witness? Write the answers to the questions about the photo on page 52. Then ask your partner the questions, and write the answers. Do *not* look back at the photo.

	You	Your partner
1. How many women are there?	....	....
2. What is the man on the far left doing?	....	....
3. What color is the carpet?	....	....
4. How many pictures are on the walls?	....	....
5. Which of the people is wearing a necktie?	....	....

Compare your answers. Then look back at the photo to check your answers.

Task 27

Your partner is going to visit one of the cities described below, but needs more information before making a choice. Answer your partner's questions about the cities. Then ask your partner to choose a city to visit and to explain his or her choice.

NEW ORLEANS, LOUISIANA, U.S.A.
Average temperature **January** 12°C/54°F **June** 28°C/82°F
Food specialties *Gumbo*: a spicy soup thickened with okra *Jambalaya*: rice cooked with chicken, shrimp, or oysters and seasoned with herbs
Tourist attractions *French Quarter*: a bustling area known for gourmet food and nightlife *Garden District*: architecturally rich area perfect for bicycling *Aquarium of the Americas*: one of the best displays of marine life in the United States

RIO DE JANEIRO, BRAZIL
Average temperature **January** 27°C/81°F **June** 24°C/75°F
Food specialties *Feijoada:* a stew made of meat and black beans *Farofa*: flour cooked in butter with chopped olives, bacon, and hard-boiled eggs
Tourist attractions *Copacabana Beach*: a beautiful beach near hotels and restaurants *National Park of Tijuca*: one of the largest city parks in the world *Native American Museum*: artifacts such as clothing, jewelry, and tools

Now it's your turn. You want to visit one of the cities pictured below, but need to find out more information before making your choice.

Seoul, South Korea

Venice, Italy

Ask your partner questions about:

the weather   popular foods   popular tourist sights

What's the weather like in Seoul?

After you find out about the cities, choose the one you would most like to visit.

Task 28 Imagine that the events below happened to both of you a long time ago. Using the pictures, talk about what happened. Add as many additional details as possible.

I'll never forget the time we went to the mountains. Do you remember that?

How could I forget? I'll never forget that bus ride. It was . . .

Join another pair. Tell them what happened.

Task 29 Read these jokes and make sure you understand them. Then take turns telling them.

Teacher: If you had $5, and you asked your dad for $5, how much would you have?
Student: Um . . . $5.
Teacher: You don't know your math!
Student: You don't know my dad!

Two goats are eating garbage. One goat finds an old roll of film and chews it up.
Goat 1: Did you enjoy the film?
Goat 2: Actually, I preferred the book.

Do you know any jokes? Tell one to your group.

Task 30 Think of a funny story to explain the photo below. Answer these questions.

- Who are the people in the photo?
- How did the man end up in that situation?
- What's going to happen next?

Tell your story to your group.

Task 31 Walk around the classroom, and find one person who answers YES to each question. Then ask an additional question to get more information. Write the person's name and the additional information. Try to get a different student's name for each question.

Do you have a part-time job, Wendy?

Yes, I do.

Who . . . ?	Name	Additional information
1. has a part-time job		
2. has a younger brother		
3. plays a musical instrument		
4. collects something unusual as a hobby		

When you finish, rejoin your group. Tell them what you learned about your classmates.

Wendy has a part-time job. She works at . . .

Task 32 Read the descriptions of the two jobs, and then close your book. Describe the jobs to your group without mentioning the job titles. Ask your group to guess which jobs you're talking about.

This person takes an actor's place when a scene in a movie is too dangerous. Jumping off buildings and driving cars very fast are just some of the things that he or she does. This is the most dangerous job in film production, and safety classes are required. **(stuntperson)**

This person begins work after the movie has been filmed. He or she looks at the film and decides which parts of the movie to cut because they are too long or boring. This person uses a special machine to cut out pieces of film and put other pieces together. **(film editor)**

Task 33 Take turns playing these word games. Read the rules and explain them to your group.

Movie charades

Think of a movie. Act out the movie title without saying anything.

The others guess what the movie is. The first person to guess correctly is the winner. That person then acts out a movie title.

Task 34 Look at these photos. Work together and try to guess what the products do. How do you think they work?

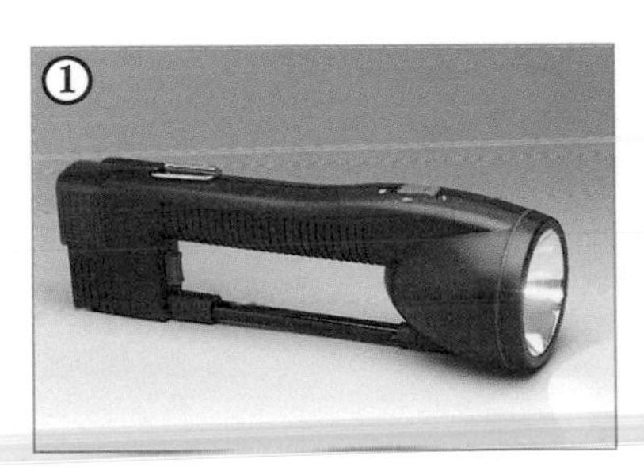

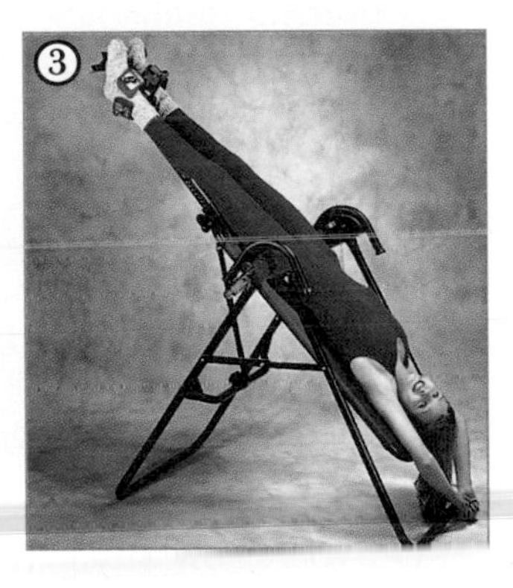

Each person in your group has a description of one of the items above. Take turns asking and answering questions about the products. Find out as much information as you can.

HANG UPS™ Heavy Duty Inversion Table

Fight stress and back pain with Hang Ups™ Heavy Duty Inversion Table. Strap yourself into the ankle holders and move into a comfortable position. An adjustable strap stops the table at any position.

Hang Ups™ Heavy Duty Inversion Table comes with an instructional video and a 90-page book, *Better Back, Better Body*. Holds up to 300 pounds.

$399.95

What is it used for?

Task 35 Think of a funny story to explain the photo below. Answer these questions.

- Who are the people in the photo?
- How did the woman on the left end up in that situation?
- What's going to happen next?

Tell your story to your group.

Task 36 Read these jokes and make sure you understand them. Then take turns telling them.

Teacher: If I had three oranges in one hand and four oranges in the other, what would I have?
Student: Very big hands!

Patient: How can I live to be 100?
Doctor: Give up cookies, cake, and ice cream. Stop eating red meat and bread – and no soft drinks.
Patient: And if I do all of that, will I live to be 100?
Doctor: Maybe not, but it will certainly seem like it!

Do you know any jokes? Tell one to your group.

Task 37 Take turns. Choose a painting and describe it in terms of color, mood, and style. Have your partner guess the painting you're describing.

color	**style**	**mood**
bright/subtle	abstract/figurative	happy/sad
varied/similar	classic/modern	peaceful/tense
vibrant/dull		romantic/unromantic

American Gothic by Grant Wood, Friends of the American Art Collection, Art Institute of Chicago/SuperStock

Amedeo Modigliani, *Bride and Groom (The Couple).* Museum of Modern Art, NY/Lerner Collection/SuperStock

Jan Van Eyck, *The Arnolfini Marriage.* National Gallery, London/SuperStock

Appendix

Activity 1A
page 22

The jobs are:

1. c	3. b	5. d
2. f	4. a	6. e

Activity 2B
page 23

The answers are:

1. opening and closing an umbrella
2. blowing through a straw into water
3. scratching paper with a paper clip
4. squeezing a bag of flour

Activity 2A
page 29

The answers are:

do aerobics
play badminton
play baseball
play basketball
go bowling
go cycling
go fishing
play football
play golf
do gymnastics
play hockey
go ice-skating
go jogging
do judo
do karate
go roller-skating
go sailing
go skiing
play soccer
do sumo wrestling
go surfing
go swimming
do tae kwon do
play tennis
play volleyball
go walking
do weight lifting
go windsurfing

Activity 2C
page 29

Look at the chart below to find out what your score means.

Participating in sports

less than 25: You aren't an active person. You avoid playing sports whenever possible.
26–50: You're somewhat active, but not what we'd call a sports nut.
51–150: You're an active person, and you like playing a lot of different sports.
151–250: You're a sports nut. You've tried a lot of different sports and still spend a lot of time exercising.
over 250: Wow! You must be a professional athlete! (Or maybe you added your numbers up wrong!)

Watching sports

less than 10: You *really* hate watching sports.
11–50: You like sports, but you don't watch them that often.
51–100: You're a sports fan. You really enjoy watching different sports.
101–150: You're a sports nut. Sports are a very important part of your life.
over 150: Hmm, this is a very high score. Do you think sports may be taking over your life? Do you have time for anything else?

Activity 1C *page 38*

All three photos show Australia.

Activity 1B *page 40*

All can be found in New Zealand.

Activity 2B *page 41*

The items are:

1. h	5. a	9. g
2. j	6. f	10. c
3. i	7. k	11. e
4. b	8. l	12. d

Activity 1B *page 48*

The interpretation of your quiz score is:

Score	
12–23	You're so green, it's unbelievable! Are there even more things you do to protect the environment?
24–35	You're very environmentally aware. You care about and respect the world around you.
36–47	You do some things to protect the environment, but there's always room for improvement.
48–60	You're not green at all. Be aware of the things you can do and try. Everything you do will help.

Activity 1C *page 61*

The art and artists are:

1. *Male Torso* by Fernando Botero (1992)
2. *Autumn, or The Grapes Brought from the Promised Land* by Nicolas Poussin (circa 1660)
3. *Red Poppy* by Georgia O'Keeffe (1927)
4. *Galloping Horse* by Xu Beihong (circa 1950)
5. *Broadway Boogie Woogie* by Piet Mondrian (1942–1943)
6. *The Two Fridas* by Frida Kahlo (1939)

Activity 1E *page 63*

The musical instruments are:

1. violin	5. piano
2. guitar	6. cello
3. drums	7. saxophone
4. flute	8. clarinet

Activity 1 *page 66*

The buildings and dates are:

Taj Mahal, 1648	Notre Dame, 1250
Kiyomizu Temple, 1633	Empire State Building, 1931
Colosseum, 82 B.C.	Parthenon, 432 B.C.
Petronas Towers, 1996	St. Mark's, 537

Self-study

Dear student,

The following section is for use with the Self-study CD. These listening activities will give you an opportunity to improve your listening comprehension at home. The listening sections you'll hear on the CD come directly from the 16 units in *Let's Talk 2* Student's Book. You can use these pages on your own if you have difficulty with an activity in class or just want additional listening practice.

When you see * in a lesson, you know that you can also hear the same listening on the Self-study CD. Usually the whole passage is on the CD, but sometimes only part is included.

Important: Do not listen to the Self-study CD for a lesson until after you study the lesson in class. However, after the lesson you may listen as many times as you'd like. You can check your answers beginning on page 108.

A separate grammar reference section is also included. Look at this section if you have particular grammar questions or problems.

Self-study

Self-study

Unit 1

Track 2

A Listen to the four conversations. Check (✔) the sentences you hear.

1. ☑ How do you like this class?
   ☐ How do you find this class?

2. ☑ Do you work here?
   ☐ Do you work around here?

3. ☑ Really, it's no trouble at all.
   ☐ It's really no trouble at all.

4. ☐ I think I've seen you around here before.
   ☑ I don't think I've seen you around here before.

Track 3

B Listen to the four conversations again. Fill in the missing words.

1. Woman 1: Yeah, I had the same teacher last year. She is a little ......tough...... [1] .
   Woman 2: Oh, you did? Um...Are her tests hard?
   Woman 1: Her tests aren't that .... [2] if you keep up with the reading . . .

2. Man 2: Do you think I should press the emergency .... [1] ?
   Man 1: No, let's just wait a minute or two first. It may start by .... [2] again.

3. Woman 1: Hi. Excuse me,...um...do you need any help?
   Woman 2: Oh, yes, I do. I've been .... [1] around in circles. I...I can't seem to find the train station.
   Woman 1: Oh, well, I'm going in that .... [2] . You can walk with me. I'll show you where it is.

4. Woman: Excuse me, do you need a hand?
   Man: Oh, yes, please. I haven't .... [1] one like this before.
   Woman: Oh, it's...it's really quite easy. All you have to do is .... [2] the document here.
   Man: Here? OK.

Unit 2

Track 4

A Listen to the two interviews. Write **M** by the details about Michael and **A** by the details about Amy.

1. .... likes literature
2. .... likes languages
3. .... is a college student
4. .... is applying for college
5. .... would like to be a lawyer
6. .... is taking a money management class
7. .... wants to make some money someday
8. .... would consider working abroad

Track 5

B Listen again to the interview with Michael. Mark the statements True (**T**) or False (**F**).

1. .... Michael dislikes most of his classes.
2. .... He enjoys reading.
3. .... His history teacher makes class fun.
4. .... He has always had great teachers.
5. .... He is good at remembering dates.
6. .... College starts in the summer.
7. .... He would like to study politics.
8. .... He hopes to be a politician someday.

Track 6

C Listen again to the first part of the interview with Amy. Correct the six mistakes.

Interviewer: So, Amy, which classes do you enjoy the most in high school?

Amy: Well, I think...um...my language classes are definitely my favorites right now.

Interviewer: Mm-hmm. Which ones are you taking?

Amy: I'm taking three. I'm studying French, Spanish, and Dutch right now.

Interviewer: Uh-huh. Why? What made you pick those three?

Amy: Well,...um...I've always loved languages – I thought Spanish would be the most interesting.

Interviewer: Uh-huh.

Amy: Uh...French is the most beautiful, I think.

Interviewer: Mm-hmm.

Amy: And...uh...I met...uh...someone from Denmark a couple of months ago and loved the language, and I decided to study that, too.

Interviewer: That's terrific. Do you ever get them confused in your mind while you're writing?

Amy: Sometimes. Yeah, sometimes I mix them up, and it's a disaster!

Unit 3
Track 7

A Read Tony's description of his favorite recipe. Fill in the blanks with the best words from the box. Then listen and check your answers.

serve	place	pour	marinate	steam	heat	garnish	chop

Oh, I'm a big seafood lover, and the favorite dish is steamed flounder with ginger and scallions. I always start off with the freshest flounder I could buy. And I .... (1) it in soy sauce overnight. Then I place it in a steamer, and .... (2) it for about three to four minutes. I .... (3) up some fresh scallion and some julienned ginger slices, and .... (4) it on top of the fish, and let it steam for about another three to four minutes. On a separate pan, I take a little bit of vegetable oil, and .... (5) it up. When the fish is ready to be taken out of the steamer, I .... (6) the hot oil all over the fish with the ginger and scallion. Then I .... (7) it with a little parsley, and I .... (8) it hot to my guests.

Track 8

B Listen to Wanda describing her favorite recipe. Correct the seven mistakes.

Hi! My name is Wanda, and I'm from California, and my favorite dish is "Mama Pearl's double-seasoned fried chicken." You take some chicken pieces, and you dry them off, and...season them with garlic salt, garlic powder, thyme, oregano, and a little seasoned pepper if you like. Then you put the chicken aside. Take a brown paper bag, put it – fill it full with flour, and season it with the same seasoning that you seasoned your chicken with. Take the chicken pieces, put it inside the brown paper bag, close the top, hold it, and shake it so that the flour and the seasoning goes all the way through the chicken. Then you take a cast-iron skillet, and you fill it with vegetable oil, and you make sure the oil is really, really hot. Don't let it boil, but make sure it's hot because that's the secret. Then you take the chicken pieces, and you put it in the oil, and you turn it until it's golden brown, and when it's done, you take it out of the pot, and you place it on a brown paper bag. It's really important to drain the chicken on the brown plastic bag – it does something to the flavor. But there you have it, and all you have to do is eat – it's delicious!

Unit 4

Track 9

A Listen to Tom discussing two friends. Mark the statements True (**T**) or False (**F**).

1. ...T... Tom and Jeff are best friends.
2. .... Tom and Jeff met in middle school.
3. .... Tom and Jeff didn't become friends right away.
4. .... Jeff doesn't live near Tom anymore.
5. .... Tom and Erica work together.
6. .... Tom thinks Erica is very funny.
7. .... Tom only sees Erica at work.

Track 10

B Listen to Lori discussing two friends, and answer the questions.

1. How long have Lori and Steven been friends? ..a long time..
2. When did they meet? ....
3. What did they have in common? ....
4. How often do they see each other now? ....
5. What do they often go see together? ....
6. Where did Lori meet her newest friend? ....
7. What are they planning to do this summer? ....
8. What do they have in common? ....

Track 11

C Listen to Phyllis discussing her friend Dorothy. Fill in the missing words.

Phyllis: My oldest friend is Dorothy.

Interviewer: And how did you and Dorothy meet?

Phyllis: Well, I met Dorothy, we were about 18 years old, and she had come to New York, and she was evicted from her apartment. She couldn't pay the ....rent........ (1), and so I said, "Well, why don't you .... (2) in with me?" I had an apartment with an .... (3) room, and that's how we met. We've been friends since then. She's been there for me, and I've been there for her, and she's just a lot of fun.

Interviewer: What kinds of things do you do when you're together?

Phyllis: Well, we sit around, we talk about .... (4) times, we gossip about a lot of friends that we have in common. Uh...She's a wonderful storyteller, and so I love to hear her stories, and she's a fashion designer, so we talk about .... (5) and politics and a lot of things. We have a lot in common.

Unit 5

Track 12

A Listen to Laura discussing her first day of work. Correct the six mistakes.

Friend: Hey, Laura. How was your day?

Laura: You know what? I had a great day. This was my first day at my new job. I...I thought it was going to be kind of a quiet place, but it was kind of noisy.

Friend: Good. How were the people?

Laura: Well, I was surprised that my boss was actually supportive and really nice. In fact, all the partners there seemed to be very nice, and they helped me in. I was worried that they might give me a little bit of an easy time because I'm young and I'm inexperienced, but they didn't.

Friend: Oh, that's great. Are you looking forward to going back tomorrow?

Laura: I really am. As a matter of fact, I'm working late tomorrow night. Can you believe it? They said on most days they would like me to spend a little bit more time there, and they do pay good overtime, so I'll make a little bit more money.

Friend: That's terrific.

Laura: That's good, right?

Friend: Yeah.

Track 13

B Read the interview of Christopher discussing his first day of work. Fill in the blanks with the best words from the box. Then listen and check your answers.

new	busy	boring	fun	complicated	impatient	friendly

Friend: Hey, how was your first day on the job?

Christopher: You know, it was really ....(1) . Yeah, I mean, I didn't think it would be as much fun as it was. I thought it was going to be kind of ....(2) , you know.

Friend: Sure. Well,...um...how was it?

Christopher: Well, let's see, I went in this morning, and I met my new boss, who is really cool, and she explained everything I needed to know, and – well, it's really not that ....(3) . The...the work part of it is really easy, you just work the machines. But what was really fun was talking to the customers. See, it takes about a minute to make the juice, and while you wait, you just get a chance to talk to the customers. And everybody was really ....(4) , and they asked me questions like "Oh, you're ....(5) here. How do you like the job?" and stuff. And even at lunch, when it got really ....(6) , everybody stayed relaxed and nobody got ....(7) if they had to wait in line.

Unit 6

Track 14

A Listen to the three interviews. Check (✔) the questions you hear.

1. ☑ What sort of interests do you have?
   ☐ What are you most interested in?

   ☐ What do you like about those activities the most?
   ☐ What do you enjoy most about those activities?

   ☐ And how long do you spend on those sort of activities?
   ☐ And how much time do you spend doing those activities?

2. ☐ What do you do in your free time?
   ☐ What are your favorite things to do in your free time?

   ☐ And what do you enjoy most about those things?
   ☐ And why do you enjoy doing those things?

   ☐ And how often do you spend doing those things?
   ☐ And how long do you get to spend on those things?

3. ☐ What hobbies do you enjoy doing?
   ☐ What sort of hobbies do you have?

   ☐ And what do you enjoy most about each activity?
   ☐ But why do you enjoy each of those activities?

   ☐ How long do you spend on each activity?
   ☐ How long have you been doing each of those activities?

Track 15

B Listen to the interviews again. Check (✔) the correct answers.

1. What does Wanda like about taking long walks?
   ☐ being competitive
   ☑ being outdoors

2. How long does Wanda walk every day?
   ☐ an hour
   ☐ two hours

3. What does Robert like to read about?
   ☐ baseball
   ☐ UFOs

4. When does Robert read?
   ☐ only on Sundays
   ☐ at night

5. What is probably Christopher's least favorite hobby?
   ☐ computers
   ☐ bird-watching

6. What does he do about four times a week?
   ☐ go to the gym
   ☐ classify birds

Unit 7

Track 16

A Listen to Lori's story. Mark the statements True (**T**) or False (**F**).

1. ...F... Lori has done yoga for many years.
2. .... She thinks yoga is slow and tranquil.
3. .... Yoga provides her with balance.
4. .... She thinks the workout is easy.

Track 17

B Listen to Terry's story. Correct the three mistakes.

Well, you know they say that swimming is the best, most total exercise because it works out your whole body. So, you know, you're not isolating any particular muscle group, your whole body's getting a workout. And it really engages your breathing very fully. So when you're done, you feel ~~sleepy~~ tired, but in a very satisfying way. It's one of the easiest ways that you can exercise because it's nonimpact. You don't hurt your bones or your muscles. Swimming is great because I...you know, I'm my own boss. I just go whenever I can squeeze it in, even for 20 minutes.

Track 18

C Listen to Robert's story. Fill in the missing words.

I'm a runner. You know, great for your ....heart.......[1] , it's great for your whole body, you get out in the sun. Every morning I run at least...uh...5 miles, and it's...uh...it's a great way to ....[2] people, too. I go to the park and, you know, you have a good time out there in the sunshine before you go to ....[3] .

Track 19

D Listen to three people's stories. Write **T** by the details about Trevor, **C** by the details about Christopher, and **B** by the details about Bill.

1. ...T... He walks a lot.
2. .... He doesn't mention exercise.
3. .... He works out with weights.
4. .... He says he doesn't have any stress.
5. .... He prefers playing with other people.

Unit 8

Track 20

A Listen to Wanda's story. Check (✔) the correct answers.

1. Where do Wanda's grandparents live?
   - ☐ in a foreign country
   - ☑ on a farm
   - ☐ with Wanda
2. What did she do there?
   - ☐ raise chickens
   - ☐ plant vegetables
   - ☐ pick apples
3. What did Wanda do at the end of the day?
   - ☐ eat and talk
   - ☐ watch TV
   - ☐ cook a big meal
4. How does she describe her stay at her grandparents' place?
   - ☐ fun but quiet
   - ☐ noisy and dirty
   - ☐ beautiful but boring

Track 21

B Listen to Robert's story. Correct the five mistakes.

My friend from ~~California~~ Canada was in town last weekend, and I showed him around. And ...uh...it was really fun. I thought it was going to be, you know, a bit of a drag, you know, taking him here and there, but...um...I ended up seeing a part of my town that I'd never seen before. Uh...We went to the park,...uh...we went to museums that I had never seen before. And...uh...we also went to the opera one night – oh, my gosh, it was just amazing, and I had never been to the opera before.

You know, when someone from out of town comes to visit, you end up doing things in your own city that you've never thought of doing before. It was really great. The only thing is...uh...if I had it all to do all over again, I probably would plan out an itinerary for exactly what we'd do on what day because some days we spent, you know, a couple of hours just trying to figure out where to go.

Track 22

C Listen to Marni's story, and answer the questions.

1. Who went on vacation? Marni's family
2. Where did Marni stay for a week? ....
3. What did she do before lunch every day? ....
4. What did she do after lunch? ....
5. What did she do every night? ....
6. What didn't she like about the week? ....

Unit 9

Track 23

A Listen to Jackie's interview. Check (✔) the questions you hear.

- ☐ When did you go there?
- ☑ When were you there?

- ☐ What's the weather like?
- ☐ What did you like about the weather?

- ☐ What did you like about the food?
- ☐ Did you like the food?

- ☐ Which part of the country would you say you liked the most?
- ☐ Which part of the country did you say you liked the best?

Track 24

B Listen to Nick's interview. Mark the statements True (**T**) or False (**F**).

1. ...T... Nick began his trip last summer.
2. .... He began his sight-seeing in the countryside.
3. .... He's not interested in sports.
4. .... His favorite part of the trip was the beautiful islands.
5. .... He enjoyed staying with his relatives.
6. .... He studied the language on his trip.

Track 25

C Listen to Kate's interview. Check (✔) the correct answers.

1. When did Kate go on her trip?
   - ☐ last March
   - ☐ a year ago
   - ☑ 2 years ago

2. What was the weather like?
   - ☐ mostly sunny
   - ☐ mostly rainy
   - ☐ mostly cloudy

3. What kind of museums did she visit?
   - ☐ history museums
   - ☐ craft museums
   - ☐ art museums

4. What did she visit?
   - ☐ the capital city
   - ☐ a mountain city
   - ☐ a silver mine

5. What did she buy there?
   - ☐ a bracelet
   - ☐ gold jewelry
   - ☐ a silver ring

Unit 10
Track 26

A Read the conversation between Tony and a salesclerk. Fill in the blanks with the best words from the box. Then listen and check your answers.

more	long	light	expensive	good	heavier	silver	sale

Clerk: Can I help you?

Tony: Yes, please,...uh...I-I want to look at these CD players. Can you tell me about that one please? Is it ....expensive.... (1) ?

Clerk: Oh, no, it's on .... (2) this week. It's $20 off the listed price.

Tony: Oh, great. Oh, wow, it's really .... (3) , too. I just – I thought it would be .... (4) .

Clerk: No, it's one of the lightest ones we have. And it has a very .... (5) battery life. One set will last 10 hours, or you can use rechargeable batteries. Uh...The anti-shock feature is .... (6) , too. If you're playing it while you're jogging, for example, it absolutely won't skip.

Tony: Oh, great, because I know some of them do. But does this one pick up FM radio as well? You see, I like listening to the radio on the headphones sometimes.

Clerk: Um...no, it doesn't. You'd have to pay a lot .... (7) for that. Not many models have a radio built in.

Tony: Hmm. Well, does it come in any other colors? I really don't like the .... (8) .

Clerk: No it's only in silver.

Tony: Oh. Well, I...I'm going to have to think about it. Thank you.

Clerk: You're welcome.

Track 27

B Listen to the conversation between Georgia and a salesclerk. Mark the statements True (**T**) or False (**F**).

1. ...T... There's only one camcorder in stock.
2. .... The price is $599 plus tax.
3. .... It's a very famous brand.
4. .... It's small and lightweight.
5. .... Georgia doesn't like the design.
6. .... Georgia decides not to buy the camcorder.

Track 28

C Listen to the conversation between Tim and a salesclerk, and answer the questions.

1. How much is the sale price of the computer? ...$999..............................
2. What color is the computer? ...blue...
3. How long does the battery last on one charge under normal use? ....
4. What isn't already installed? ....
5. What impresses Tim about the computer? ....

Unit 11

Track 29

A Listen to the five conversations. Check (✔) the reasons the people say they want to throw the things away.

1. ☑ We don't need them anymore.
   ☐ We don't have room for them anymore.
2. ☐ It's broken.
   ☐ It's chipped.
3. ☐ It's been used already.
   ☐ It's been written on already.
4. ☐ It's dirty.
   ☐ It's empty.
5. ☐ I've finished what I was eating.
   ☐ I've finished what I was writing.

Track 30

B Read these parts of the five conversations. Fill in the blanks with the best words from the box. Then listen and check your answers.

unfold	get	freeze	keep	cut	put	buy	cover	reuse	wrap	use

1. Well, yeah, but you can use them again. Sure. See, what I do sometimes is I take them, and I ....1............ them up into smaller pieces. It makes great note paper to leave by the phone. Or you can also ....2............ the other side of each page. It works great.

2. Well, I-I know it's chipped, but it's still OK. I mean, there are a lot of other things you could ....1............ it for. You know, you could put...um...pens and pencils in it and ....2............ it on your desk. Or another idea is you could put flowers in it and use it as a vase.

3. Well, you ....1............ new label and put it on top of the old address, and then you can ....2............ a bigger stamp and put it on top of the old stamp.

4. Yeah, but you can use it again. It's great for storage. You can ....1............ leftovers in there and ....2............ them. Or you can put cookies in there – with the plastic lid on, they keep really fresh.

5. Yeah, but you can use that again. You know, you just ....1............ it, make it flat, and you can ....2............ your food with it, or you could wrap your lunch in it, or you could ....3............ a saucepan with it. I mean, there are lots of uses for that stuff.

Unit 12

Track 31

A Listen to story 1. Mark the statements True (**T**) or False (**F**).

1. ...T... The forest fires started burning on Friday.
2. .... Thousands of families in Bellevue had to leave the area.
3. .... The fire remains out of control.
4. .... The fire will probably not get any closer to the city.

Track 32

B Listen to story 2. Number the events in order from 1 to 8.

.... The stomach pains became worse.
.... A friend radioed for help.
...1.... Mary went out on her boat.
.... She had an operation.
.... She is recovering.
.... She was taken to the hospital.
.... A helicopter was sent out.
.... She began to have stomach pains.

Track 33

C Listen to story 3. Number the events in order from 1 to 9.

.... People came to see the whale.
.... The divers calmed the whale down.
.... The whale got confused and couldn't leave at high tide.
.... The whale tried to swim out of the bay.
.... They guided the whale out of the bay.
.... Noise scared the whale.
...1.... A whale swam into the bay.
.... The tide went out.
.... A team of divers arrived.

Track 34

D Listen to story 4, and answer the questions.

1. Where did the reunion take place? ....Chicago's O'Hare Airport....
2. Where is Stacy Baxter from? ....
3. How old are Stacy and Alicia? ....
4. When did Stacy know she had a twin sister? ....
5. When did Stacy know her sister's name? ....
6. How did Stacy get in touch with her sister? ....

Unit 13
Track 35

A Listen to the conversation. Check (✔) the adjectives you hear.

- [ ] late
- [x] free
- [ ] new
- [ ] terrific
- [ ] interesting
- [ ] good
- [ ] great
- [ ] fantastic
- [ ] wonderful
- [ ] quieter
- [ ] peaceful
- [ ] better
- [ ] relaxed
- [ ] best
- [ ] old
- [ ] fair
- [ ] gorgeous
- [ ] fun
- [ ] warm
- [ ] happy

Track 36

B Listen to the conversation again. Fill in the missing words.

Kevin: Hello.

Jeffrey: Hey, Kevin. It's Jeffrey. I bet you know why I'm ......calling...... (1), huh?

Kevin: Yeah, I guess so. Look, I haven't .... (2) my mind.

Jeffrey: OK, well, the room is still free. But not for much longer. I mean, I have to find someone else to move in here if you don't want to do it.

Kevin: Oh, look, you know how I feel about .... (3) to the city.

Jeffrey: Yeah, but on the other hand, you did say you were .... (4) for a new job, and there are plenty of interesting and very good jobs in the city.

Kevin: If you say so.

Jeffrey: Hey, just .... (5) of all the great museums, right? The wonderful movies, and you got concerts, you got theaters –

Kevin: I know, I know, I know. Well, you know, it's just, it's much quieter out here, and, you know, the air is just better out here. I don't know, life is just – it's more relaxed.

Jeffrey: You sound a hundred years old.

Kevin: No, no, no, I don't think that's fair. I mean, you know how the city is at this time of year, especially with all the tourists, I mean. And you know how gorgeous it is out here, right?

Jeffrey: Yeah, I guess so, but .... (6) in the city can be so much fun. Listen, why don't you come and .... (7) with me once more, say, over the holidays, and we can .... (8) about it some more, huh?

Kevin: Uh, you know, that could be fun. OK, why don't I . . .

Unit 14
Track 37

A Listen to the movie review. Mark the statements True (**T**) or False (**F**).

1. ....T... Sally and Johnny Applegate are teenagers.
2. .... The Applegates are insects.
3. .... They want people to stop destroying their home.
4. .... They try to act like a normal family.
5. .... They eat cardboard and liquid sugar.
6. .... They begin to have problems.
7. .... *Meet the Applegates* has silly special effects.
8. .... The movie is funny but about a serious issue.
9. .... The movie has an environmental theme.

Track 38

B Listen to the review again. Correct the seven mistakes.

Meet the Applegates

The Applegates seem like many other American families. Father Dick is a security guard at a ~~research lab~~ power plant. Mother Jane is a homemaker. Teenagers Sally and Johnny are smart kids. But what everyone knows is that the Applegates are really insects! They come from the Amazon rain forest and have disguised themselves as humans so that they can advertise a campaign to stop people from destroying their home.

While they're planning their campaign, the Applegates try to learn about America and act like a normal family (which isn't easy, since they only eat garbage and liquid sugar!). But they soon have problems. Jane starts charging too much on her new credit cards, and both Johnny and Sally get into trouble. Dick has trouble with his mother-in-law. But thankfully, Aunt Bea Applegate arrives to save the day!

Packed with clever special effects, witty observations, and plenty of music, *Meet the Applegates* is a funny film with an environmental theme.

Unit 15
Track 39

A Listen to Phil's interview. Correct the seven mistakes.

Interviewer: Phil, what do you remember about being 12 years old?

Phil: Well, when I was 12 years old, my family was very poor, and we lived in this tiny ~~house~~ apartment downtown with...uh...three younger sisters and one older brother, and we all slept in the same bedroom on bunk beds.

I was a big collector of comic books when I was 12. I used to collect all the Superman and Batman comic books, used to run to the store every Thursday when they came out, and they'd cost about 20 cents back then. And all the friends would get together, and we'd go to the corner store and buy comic books, and then head back for the playground and spend the next hour reading comics and...and selling them and...and just talking about them.

Interviewer: So what was the best thing about being 12?

Phil: Well, my grandmother would spoil me because I was the baby, and I would always get more toys than they ever did. I would also get to buy whatever I wanted to. Um...It was also a time when I knew that if I got into any kind of trouble...uh...in the neighborhood that my older sisters and my cousin would come and protect me.

Track 40

B Listen to Wanda's interview. Check (✔) the things she liked to do.

- [x] play tag
- [ ] play hopscotch
- [ ] jump rope
- [ ] chase boys
- [ ] take responsibility
- [ ] tell stories
- [ ] play dress-up
- [ ] read
- [ ] go to plays
- [ ] study at museums

Track 41

C Listen to Tom's interview, and answer the questions.

1. Where did Tom go on his first "date"? to a dance
2. How did he get there? ....
3. What did Tom's father start to call him? ....
4. What sports did Tom play? ....

Unit 16

Track 42

A Listen to story 1. Check (✔) the correct answers.

1. Who came to the woman's house?
   - [x] some repairmen
   - [ ] some salesmen
   - [ ] some deliverymen

2. Where did the woman go?
   - [ ] to a pet shop
   - [ ] to a store
   - [ ] to a hardware store

3. Where was the bird cage?
   - [ ] in the living room
   - [ ] in the kitchen
   - [ ] in the dining room

4. What did the woman do when she came home?
   - [ ] screamed
   - [ ] died
   - [ ] passed out

Track 43

B Listen to story 2. Number the events in order from 1 to 10.

.... They reported the theft to the police.
.... They went to work.
.... Someone stole everything from the house.
...1.... Someone took a couple's car.
.... They went to a Broadway show.
.... They read the note on the car.
.... They found the car in the driveway.
.... They returned home from the show.
.... They returned from work.
.... The couple woke up one morning.

Track 44

C Listen to story 3, and answer the questions.

1. Who is the speaker talking about? ....his brother-in-law..........
2. Where was he? ....
3. What was the woman carrying? ....
4. Where did she put her purse? ....
5. Where did she put her groceries? ....
6. What did the other man scream at the woman? ....
7. What pulled out in front of the woman? ....
8. How was the baby? ....

Self-study answer key

Unit 1

A

1. How do you like this class?
2. Do you work here?
3. Really, it's no trouble at all.
4. I don't think I've seen you around here before.

B

1. 1. tough
   2. bad
2. 1. button
   2. itself
3. 1. walking
   2. direction
4. 1. used
   2. place

Unit 2

A

1. M
2. A
3. A
4. M
5. M
6. A
7. M
8. A

B

1. F
2. T
3. T
4. F
5. F
6. F
7. T
8. F

C

1. enjoy the most in ~~high school~~	enjoy the most in college
2. are ~~definitely~~ my favorites	are probably my favorites
3. French, Spanish, and ~~Dutch~~	French, Spanish, and Danish
4. be the most ~~interesting~~	be the most useful
5. a couple of ~~months~~ ago	a couple of years ago
6. while you're ~~writing~~	while you're studying

Unit 3

A

1. marinate
2. steam
3. chop
4. place
5. heat
6. pour
7. garnish
8. serve

B

1. from ~~California~~	from New York City
2. you ~~dry~~ them off	you wash them off
3. a little seasoned ~~pepper~~	a little seasoned salt
4. fill it ~~full~~ with flour	fill it halfway with flour
5. fill it with ~~vegetable~~ oil	fill it with peanut oil
6. Don't let it ~~boil~~	Don't let it smoke
7. on a brown ~~plastic~~ bag	on a brown paper bag

Unit 4

A

1. T
2. F
3. F
4. T
5. T
6. T
7. F

B

1. a long time/many years
2. in high school
3. music
4. every couple of weeks
5. concerts
6. at the theater
7. go camping
8. hard work and travel

C

1. rent
2. move
3. extra
4. old
5. clothes

Unit 5

A

1. kind of a ~~quiet~~ place	kind of a dull place
2. it was kind of ~~noisy~~	it was kind of fun
3. and they ~~helped~~ me in	and they welcomed me in
4. a little bit of ~~an easy~~ time	a little bit of a hard time
5. ~~young~~ and I'm inexperienced	new and I'm inexperienced
6. said on ~~most~~ days	said on some days

B

1. fun
2. boring
3. complicated
4. friendly
5. new
6. busy
7. impatient

Unit 6

A

1. What sort of interests do you have?
   What do you enjoy most about those activities?
   And how long do you spend on those sort of activities?

2. What do you do in your free time?
   And what do you enjoy most about those things?
   And how long do you get to spend on those things?

3. What sort of hobbies do you have?
   And what do you enjoy most about each activity?
   How long do you spend on each activity?

B

1. being outdoors
2. two hours
3. UFOs
4. at night
5. computers
6. go to the gym

Unit 7

A

1. F
2. T
3. T
4. F

B

1. you feel ~~sleepy~~	you feel tired
2. one of the ~~easiest~~ ways	one of the safest ways
3. even for ~~20~~ minutes	even for ~~10~~ minutes

C

1. heart
2. meet
3. work

D

1. T
2. B
3. C
4. T
5. C

Unit 8

A

1. on a farm
2. pick apples
3. eat and talk
4. fun but quiet

B

1. friend from ~~California~~	friend from Canada
2. in town last ~~weekend~~	in town last week
3. went to the ~~park~~	went to the zoo
4. it was just ~~amazing~~	it was just beautiful
5. figure out ~~where to go~~	figure out what to do

C

1. Marni's family
2. in her apartment
3. study
4. go jogging or swimming
5. go to the movies
6. doing the cooking and cleaning

Unit 9

A

When were you there?
What's the weather like?
Did you like the food?
Which part of the country would you say you liked the most?

B

1. T
2. F
3. F
4. F
5. T
6. F

C

1. 2 years ago
2. mostly sunny
3. art museums
4. a mountain city
5. a bracelet

Unit 10

A

1. expensive
2. sale
3. light
4. heavier
5. long
6. good
7. more
8. silver

B

1. T
2. F
3. F
4. T
5. F
6. F

C

1. $999
2. blue
3. 6 hours
4. software
5. the DVD feature

Unit 11

A

1. We don't need them anymore.
2. It's chipped.
3. It's been used already.
4. It's empty.
5. I've finished what I was eating.

B

1. 1. cut
   2. reuse
2. 1. use
   2. keep
3. 1. get
   2. buy
4. 1. put
   2. freeze
5. 1. unfold
   2. wrap
   3. cover

Unit 12

A

1. T
2. F
3. F
4. T

B

3 The stomach pains became worse.
4 A friend radioed for help.
1 Mary went out on her boat.
7 She had an operation.
8 She is recovering.
6 She was taken to the hospital.
5 A helicopter was sent out.
2 She began to have stomach pains.

C

4 People came to see the whale.
8 The divers calmed the whale down.
6 The whale got confused and couldn't leave at high tide.
3 The whale tried to swim out of the bay.
9 They guided the whale out of the bay.
5 Noise scared the whale.
1 A whale swam into the bay.
2 The tide went out.
7 A team of divers arrived.

D

1. Chicago's O'Hare Airport
2. Seattle, Washington
3. 45
4. 4 years ago
5. last month
6. She called her.

Unit 13

A

free
new
interesting
good
great
wonderful
quieter
better
relaxed
old
fair
gorgeous
fun

B

1. calling
2. changed
3. moving
4. looking
5. think
6. living
7. stay
8. talk

Unit 14

A

1. T
2. T
3. T
4. T
5. F
6. T
7. F
8. T
9. T

B

1. security guard at a ~~research lab~~	security guard at a power plant
2. Sally and Johnny are ~~smart~~ kids	Sally and Johnny are great kids
3. what ~~everyone~~ knows	what no one knows
4. they can ~~advertise~~ a campaign	they can start a campaign
5. try to ~~learn about America~~	try to make friends
6. trouble with his ~~mother in law~~	trouble with his boss
7. and plenty of ~~music~~	and plenty of humor

Unit 15

A

1. lived in this tiny ~~house~~ — lived in this tiny apartment
2. three ~~younger~~ sisters — three older sisters
3. they'd cost about ~~20~~ cents — they'd cost about 10 cents
4. and ~~selling~~ them — and exchanging them
5. my ~~grandmother~~ would spoil me — my mother would spoil me
6. get to ~~buy~~ whatever I wanted — get to eat whatever I wanted
7. older sisters and my ~~cousin~~ — older sisters and my brother

B

play tag
play hopscotch
jump rope
chase boys
tell stories
play dress-up

C

1. to a dance
2. His mother drove him.
3. "pal"
4. baseball, basketball, and football

Unit 16

A

1. some repairmen
2. to a store
3. in the living room
4. passed out

B

3 They reported the theft to the police.
4 They went to work.
9 Someone stole everything from the house.
1 Someone took a couple's car.
8 They went to a Broadway show.
7 They read the note on the car.
6 They found the car in the driveway.
10 They returned home from the show.
5 They returned from work.
2 The couple woke up one morning.

C

1. his brother-in-law
2. at the supermarket
3. her baby, purse, and groceries
4. on top of the car
5. in the car
6. "Hey, lady! Hey, lady!"
7. a delivery truck
8. fine, but crying

Grammar

REVIEW: SIMPLE PRESENT TENSE

Wh- questions

What	**do**	I you we they	**do** for a living?
	does	he she	

How	**does**	it	**fit**?

Affirmative statements

I You We They	**work**	in a bank.
He She	**works**	

It	**fits**	well.

Negative statements

I You We They	**don't**	**like** it.
He She	**doesn't**	

It	**doesn't**	**look** good.

Yes/No questions

Do	I you we they	**want** a new job?
Does	he she	

Does	it	**feel** OK?

Short answers

Yes, **I do**. / No, **I don't**.
Yes, **you do**. / No, **you don't**.
Yes, **we do**. / No, **we don't**.
Yes, **they do**. / No, **they don't**.
Yes, **he does**. / No, **he doesn't**.
Yes, **she does**. / No, **she doesn't**.

Yes, **it does**. / No, **it doesn't**.

Contractions

don't = do not
doesn't = does not

REVIEW: PRESENT CONTINUOUS TENSE

Wh- questions

What	**am**	I	**doing** right now?
	are	you	
	is	he she	
	are	we they	

What	**is**	it	**doing** outside?

Affirmative statements

I	**'m**	**watching** TV.
You	**'re**	
He She	**'s**	
We They	**'re**	

It	**'s**	**raining**.

Negative statements

I	**'m not**	**reading**.
You	**aren't**	
He She	**isn't**	
We They	**aren't**	

It	**isn't**	**snowing**.

Yes/No questions

Am	I	**having** fun?
Are	you	
Is	he she	
Are	we they	

Is	it	**working**?

Short answers

Yes, **I am**. / No, **I'm not**.
Yes, **you are**. / No, **you aren't**.
Yes, **he is**. / No, **he isn't**.
Yes, **she is**. / No, **she isn't**.
Yes, **we are**. / No, **we aren't**.
Yes, **they are**. / No, **they aren't**.

Yes, **it is**. / No, **it isn't**.

SIMPLE PAST OF *BE*

Wh- questions

Where	**was**	I he she	last night?
	were	you we they	

Affirmative statements

I He She	**was**	at the library.
You We They	**were**	

Negative statements

I He She	**wasn't**	home.
You We They	**weren't**	

Yes/No questions

Was	I he she	here yesterday?
Were	you we they	

Short answers

Yes, **I was**. / No, **I wasn't**.
Yes, **he was**. / No, **he wasn't**.
Yes, **she was**. / No, **she wasn't**.
Yes, **you were**. / No, **you weren't**.
Yes, **we were**. / No, **we weren't**.
Yes, **they were**. / No, **they weren't**.

Contractions

wasn't = was not

weren't = were not

SIMPLE PAST TENSE

Wh- questions

What movie	**did**	I you he she we they	**see**	last night?
How long	**did**	it	**rain**	last night?

More Wh- questions

Where did you grow up?

When did you get that jacket?

What happened?

Where did she live as a child?

What did you do last night?

Which games did you play as a child?

Who did you go to the movie with?

Affirmative statements

I You He She We They	**loved** board games.

Negative statements

I You He She We They	**didn't like** tile games.

Contraction

didn't = did not

Yes/No questions

Did	I you he she we they	**enjoy** card games?

Short answers

Yes, **I did**. / No, **I didn't**.
Yes, **you did**. / No, **you didn't**.
Yes, **he did**. / No, **he didn't**.
Yes, **she did**. / No, **she didn't**.
Yes, **we did**. / No, **we didn't**.
Yes, **they did**. / No, **they didn't**.

Some verbs are irregular in the simple past. See the Irregular Verb list on page 121.

PAST CONTINUOUS TENSE

Wh- questions

What	**was**	I he she	**doing** when the fire started?
	were	you we they	

Affirmative statements

I He She	**was**	**cooking.**
You We They	**were**	

Negative statements

I He She	**wasn't**	**ironing.**
You We They	**weren't**	

Yes/No questions

Was	I he she	**walking** to work when the fire started?
Were	you we they	

Was	it	**raining** at midnight last night?

Short answers

Yes, **I was.** / No, **I wasn't.**
Yes, **he was.** / No, **he wasn't.**
Yes, **she was.** / No, **she wasn't.**
Yes, **you were.** / No, **you weren't.**
Yes, **we were.** / No, **we weren't.**
Yes, **they were.** / No, **they weren't.**

Yes, **it was.** / No, **it wasn't.**

PAST CONTINUOUS VS. SIMPLE PAST

Use the past continuous to describe actions in progress in the past. Use the simple past to describe completed actions.

What **were** you **doing** when I **called**?
I **was taking** a nap. I **was having** a great dream. Then the phone **rang** and I **woke up**.

How **did** you **learn** about the fire?
I **was watching** TV when I **heard** the news. Some children **started** the fire when they **were playing** with matches.

FUTURE: *BE GOING TO*

Wh- questions

What	**am**	I	**going to do**?
	are	you	
	is	he she	
	are	we they	

Affirmative statements

I	**'m**	**going to leave** now.
You	**'re**	
He She	**'s**	
We They	**'re**	

It	**'s**	**going to rain** tomorrow.

Negative statements

I	**'m not**	**going to be** home.
You	**aren't**	
He She	**isn't**	
We They	**aren't**	

It	**isn't**	**going to be** a nice day.

Yes/No questions

Am	I	**going to be** here tomorrow?
Are	you	
Is	he she	
Are	we they	

Is	it	**going to rain** tomorrow?

Short answers

Yes, **I am.** / No, **I'm not.**
Yes, **you are.** / No, **you aren't.**
Yes, **he is.** / No, **he isn't.**
Yes, **she is.** / No, **she isn't.**
Yes, **we are.** / No, **we aren't.**
Yes, **they are.** / No, **they aren't.**

Yes, **it is.** / No, **it isn't.**

FUTURE: *WILL*

Wh- questions

Where	**will**	I you he she we they	**be** 10 years from now?
What	**will**	it	**be** like tomorrow?

More Wh- questions

Who will win the next election?

What time will you be home tonight?

How will the world be different 20 years from now?

How long will you be away?

How will you pay your rent?

How many people will be there?

Affirmative statements

I You He She We They	**'ll be** right here.
It	**will be** sunny.

Negative statements

I You He She We They	**won't finish** school until 2007.
It	**won't be** cloudy.

Contractions

I'll = I will

you'll = you will

he'll = he will

she'll = she will

we'll = we will

they'll = they will

won't = will not

Yes/No questions

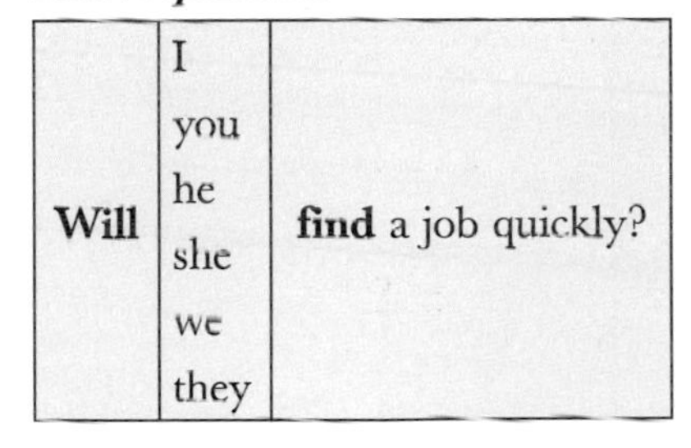

Will	I you he she we they	**find** a job quickly?

Short answers

Yes, **I will.** / No, **I won't.**
Yes, **you will.** / No, **you won't.**
Yes, **he will.** / No, **he won't.**
Yes, **she will.** / No, **she won't.**
Yes, **we will.** / No, **we won't.**
Yes, **they will.** / No, **they won't.**

EXPRESSING FUTURE TIME

Be going to *vs.* will

Use either *be going to* or *will* to express a prediction.

Future generations	**are going to** **will**	**travel** to Mars on vacations.

Use *be going to* to express a plan you've decided on. Use *will* with *maybe*, *probably*, or *I think* to express a possible plan before you've made a decision.

What **are** you **going to do** tonight?	**I'm going to see** a movie. I don't know. Maybe **I'll see** a movie.

Use *will* to express a willingness to do something.

I know you hate to go to the movies alone. **I'll go** with you.

Present continuous as future

You can use the present continuous when you're talking about a planned event or a definite intention.

What **are** you **doing** after class today?	**I'm going** to the library.

PRESENT PERFECT TENSE

Wh- questions

How long	**have**	I you we they	**been** here?
	has	he she	

How long	**has**	it	**been** sunny?

More Wh- questions

Where have you been?
What has just happened here?
What have you been up to lately?
What movies have you seen recently?
How many English courses have you taken?
Why have you been so sad lately?
How long have you lived here?

Affirmative statements

I You We They	**'ve**	**been** here for a few minutes.
He She	**'s**	

It	**'s**	**been** sunny for an hour.

Negative statements

I You We They	**haven't**	**been** here long.
He She	**hasn't**	

It	**hasn't**	**been** cloudy for an hour.

Contractions

I've = I have
you've = you have
we've = we have
they've = they have
he's = he has
she's = she has
it's = it has
haven't = have not
hasn't = has not

Yes/No questions

Have	I you we they	(ever) **gone** bungee jumping?
Has	he she	

Has	it	(ever) **snowed** here?

Short answers

Yes, **I have**. / No, **I haven't**.
Yes, **you have**. / No, **you haven't**.
Yes, **we have**. / No, **we haven't**.
Yes, **they have**. / No, **they haven't**.
Yes, **he has**. / No, **he hasn't**.
Yes, **she has**. / No, **she hasn't**.

Yes, **it has**. / No, **it hasn't**.

Many verbs have the same simple past and past participle forms.

We **talked** on the phone yesterday.	We **have talked** twice this week.

Some verbs are irregular. See the Irregular Verb list on page 121.

We **spoke** on the phone yesterday.	We **have spoken** twice this week.

We often use the present perfect with *just, already, yet, for,* and *since.*

Have you **had** dinner yet?	Yes, **I've just finished.** Yes, **I've already eaten.** No, I **haven't eaten yet.**

How long **has** she **lived** here?	She**'s lived** here **for** many years. She**'s lived** here **since** 1999.

PRESENT PERFECT VS. SIMPLE PAST

Use the simple past for an activity that began and ended at a definite time in the past. Use the present perfect to express something at an indefinite time in the past or something that continues into the present.

Have you ever **visited** another country?	Yes, I **have**. I **went** to Mexico last year.
Has he **been** here long?	No, he **hasn't**. He **arrived** about ten minutes ago.

EXPRESSIONS OF QUANTITY

Some expressions of quantity are used only with count nouns and others are used only with noncount nouns. However, some expressions of quantity are used with either count or noncount nouns.

Only with count nouns

one **each** **every**	story
two **a few** **several** **many**	stories

Only with noncount nouns

a little **much**	news

With either count or noncount nouns

no **some** **a lot of** **most** **all** **lots of**	problems pollution

Both, neither, either

Use *both, neither,* and *either* to talk about two people or things. Use a plural verb form with *both (of).*

Both restaurants **are** very reasonable.

Use a singular verb form with *neither* and *either.*

Neither restaurant **is** very expensive.
Either restaurant **is** fine.

a few, a little, few, little

A few and *a little* express a positive idea (some but not many/not much). *Few* and *little* express a more negative idea (not many/not much).

There are **a few** reasonable restaurants downtown. Let's try Sophie's.
We have **a little** money left over. Let's eat out tonight.

There are **few** reasonable restaurants downtown. Let's go somewhere else.
We have **little** money left over. Let's stay home tonight.

COMPARISONS WITH ADJECTIVES

The comparative forms of adjectives are *-er* and *more.* Generally, use *-er* for one-syllable words and two-syllable words ending in *-y*. Use *more* for words of two syllables or more. For the superlative forms, use *-est* and *most.*

Adjective	*Comparative*	*Superlative*
cheap	cheaper	cheapest
big	bigger	biggest
noisy	noisier	noisiest

Adjective	*Comparative*	*Superlative*
expensive	more expensive	most expensive
delicious	more delicious	most delicious
comfortable	more comfortable	most comfortable

Here are two irregular adjectives.

Adjective	*Comparative*	*Superlative*
good	better	best

Adjective	*Comparative*	*Superlative*
bad	worse	worst

Which restaurant is **cheaper**, Sophie's Restaurant or Joe's Steak House?
Sophie's is **cheaper than** Joe's.

Which restaurant is **the best**: Sophie's Restaurant, Joe's Steak House, or the Seafood Shack?
I think the Seafood Shack is **the best.** It's also **the most expensive.**

ARTICLES WITH GENERIC NOUNS

Use generic nouns to make generalizations. Usually *a/an* is used with a singular generic count noun.

What is **a "typical" family** in your country?

Some exceptions include the use of *the* with musical instruments, species of animals, and inventions.

Would you like to learn how to play **the violin**?
The Chilean sea bass is becoming extinct.
Who invented **the microwave oven**?

Don't use *the* with a plural count noun or a noncount noun to make a generalization.

Cities are becoming more and more crowded.
Family life in my country has changed a lot since my parents were my age.

MODALS AND SIMILAR EXPRESSIONS

Modal verbs are followed by the base form of a verb. Never add *-s* to the verb.

Expressing ability: **can**

Can you **speak** Spanish?
Yes, I **can**, but I **can't read** it very well.

Other ways to express ability

Are you **able to come** tomorrow?

Contraction

can't = cannot

Expressing necessity: **must**

I **must get** a new passport soon.
It's a secret. You **mustn't tell** anyone.

Other ways to express necessity

I **have to go** to bed early tonight.

I **need to be** at work early tomorrow.

Contraction

mustn't = must not

Asking for and giving advice: **should**

She **should study** more for her exam.
They **shouldn't make** so much noise.

Other ways to ask for and give advice

You**'d better go** or you'll be late.

Do you think I **ought to look for** a new job?

Contractions

shouldn't = should not

'd better = had better

Hypothesizing: **would**

What **would** you **do** if your car broke down?
I **would wait** for someone to stop.
I **wouldn't leave** the car.

Contraction

wouldn't = would not

Expressing possibility: **may, might, could**

Look at the sky. It **may rain.**
That **might be** the right answer.
Someone is at the door. It **could be** Mark.

Asking for and giving permission: **can, could, may**

Can I **speak** to Bill?
Could I **use** your cell phone?
May I please **sit** down?

Asking for things: **can, could, may**

Can I **have** some more coffee?
Could I **see** this in a larger size?
May I **have** a receipt, please?

Asking people to do things: **can, could**

Can you **sign** your name?
Could you **spell** your last name, please?

Offering to do things: **can, may**

Can I **get** you some more coffee?
May I **help** you, sir?

OVERVIEW: ACTIVE VOICE VS. PASSIVE VOICE

The passive voice changes the focus of a sentence. To form a passive sentence in the present, use the present of *be* + past participle.

Active	*Passive*
Industry **damages** the environment.	The environment **is damaged** by industry.
People often **recycle** newspapers, bottles, and cans.	Newspapers, bottles, and cans **are** often **recycled**.

To form a passive sentence in the past, use the past of *be* + past participle.

Active	*Passive*
Mary Anderson **invented** the windshield wiper.	The windshield wiper **was invented** by Mary Anderson.
The Egyptians **built** the Pyramids.	The Pyramids **were built** by the Egyptians.

OVERVIEW: CONDITIONAL SENTENCES

Possible situations

Use the simple present in the *if* clause and the future in the other clause.

If it **snows** tomorrow, **I'll go** skiing.
If my parents **come** this weekend, I **won't** see you until Monday.

Hypothetical situations

Use the simple past in the *if* clause and *would* + base form of the verb in the other clause.

If I **had** more money, I **would get** a cell phone.
If you **found** a wallet on the street, what **would** you **do**?

IRREGULAR VERBS

Verb	*Simple past*	*Past participle*	*Verb*	*Simple past*	*Past participle*
be	was/were	been	know	knew	known
break	broke	broken	lose	lost	lost
buy	bought	bought	make	made	made
choose	chose	chosen	meet	met	met
come	came	come	read	read	read
do	did	done	ride	rode	ridden
drink	drank	drunk	say	said	said
drive	drove	driven	see	saw	seen
eat	ate	eaten	sleep	slept	slept
find	found	found	speak	spoke	spoken
fly	flew	flown	spend	spent	spent
give	gave	given	take	took	taken
go	went	gone	think	thought	thought
have	had	had	wear	wore	worn
hear	heard	heard	write	wrote	written

Acknowledgments

Illustrations

Paulette Bogan	71
Bruce Day	32
Carlos Castellanos	5, 14, 53
Adam Hurwitz	41, 62
Randy Jones	4, 26, 79, 85
Wally Neibart	24
© The New Yorker Collection from cartoonbank.com, all rights reserved.	70
William Waitzman	13, 21, 76, 82, 91

Photographic Credits

The author and publisher are grateful for the permission to reproduce the following photographs:

Cover Photos: background: Darrell Gulin/Corbis; *top to bottom:* Ted Kawalerski/ The Image Bank; Ghislain & Marie David de Lossy/The Image Bank; R.W. Jones/Corbis; Walter Hodges/Stone; V.C.L./FPG

2 *(left to right, top to bottom)* Lee Snider/The Image Works; Ellen Senisi/ The Image Works; Kea Publishing Services Ltd./Corbis; K. Preuss/ The Image Works

6 *(top)* Myrleen Ferguson/PhotoEdit; *(bottom)* John Henley/Corbis/ Stock Market; *(right)* Bob Daemmrich/Stock Boston

7 *(left to right)* The Image Bank; Ryan McVay/Photodisc/PictureQuest; David Hanover/Stone

9 *(top)* David Pollack/Corbis/Stock Market; *(bottom)* Randy Duchaine/Corbis/ Stock Market

15 *(top)* Paul Barton/Corbis/Stock Market; *(bottom)* Ronnie Kaufman/Corbis/Stock Market; *right)* Dick Luria/FPG

16 *(left to right)* R. Lord/The Image Works; Dick Blume/The Image Works; Bob Daemmrich/The Image Works

17 *(left to right, top to bottom)* Ron Chapple/FPG; Ron Chapple/FPG; L.O.L. Inc./FPG; Ron Chapple/FPG; Ron Chapple/FPG; Stephen Simpson/FPG

20 *(left)* Roger Werth/Woodfin Camp; *(center left)* Bob Deammrich/ Stock Boston; *(center right)* Catherine Karnow/Woodfin Camp; *(left)* David Lassman/The Image Works

22 *(left to right, top to bottom)* Randy Taylor/Liaison Agency; Michael Newman/PhotoEdit; The Everett Collection; The Kobal Collection; The Everett Collection; Forrest Anderson/Liaison Agency

23 Michael Newman/PhotoEdit

25 *(left to right, top to bottom)* David Weintraub/Stock Boston; Jim Corwin/Stock Boston; Amos Nachoum/Corbis; Rudi Von Briel/PhotoEdit; David Young-Wolff/PhotoEdit; Bob Daemmrich/Stock Boston

28 *(left to right)* Steve E. Sutton/Duomo; Duomo; Robert Holmes Photography

30 *(left to right, top to bottom)* Robert Holmes Photography; Sue Lawson/PhotoEdit; Bill Aron/PhotoEdit; George Kerrigan/Digital Eyes; Myrleen Ferguson/PhotoEdit; Tetris/Blue Planet

33 *(left to right, top to bottom)* Terry Vine/Corbis; Robert Holmes Photography; Bill Bachmann/PhotoEdit; Robert Holmes Photography

34 *(left to right)* Phyllis Picardi/Stock Boston; David Pollack Corbis/Stock Market; Mark Burnett/Stock Boston

35 *(left to right, top to bottom)* Chris Jones Corbis/Stock Market; Daimler-Chrysler/Newsmakers/Liaison Agency; David Young-Wolff/PhotoEdit; Pascal Quittemelle/Stock Boston; Alese/MortPechter/Corbis/Stock Market; Kunio Owaki Corbis/Stock Market

38 *(top)* Bowman/Leo De Wys: *(left)* John Lamb/Stone; *(right)* Randy Wells/Stone

39 *(left to right)* John Lamb/Stone; Val Corbett/Stone; Markova Corbis/Stock Market

42 *(clockwise from bottom of left corner)* Corbis; PhotoEdit; David Young-Wollf/PhotoEdit; Corbis/Stock Market; Felicia Martinez/PhotoEdit; Bob Jacobson/Corbis

44 *(left to right)* courtesy of Machina, Inc.; courtesy of The Safety Zone; courtesy of VITRA Products Inc.

45 *(top)* Innervisions; *(bottom)* John Brooks/Liaison Agency

46 *(left)* Ivan Massar/Black Star/PictureQuest; *(right)* Rex Butcher/Stone; *(bottom)* Bob Deammrich/Stock Boston/PictureQuest

47 David Bartruff/FPG

49 *(top row)* Innervisions; *(bottom row left)* Jean Miele/Corbis/Stock Market; *(bottom row center)* Chris Rogers/Corbis/Stock Market; *(bottom row right)* Mug Shots/Corbis/Stock Market

50 *(left to right, top to bottom)* AP/Wide World; Spencer Grant/Stock Boston; Stephen Rose/Liaison Agency; John Darling/Stone

51 *(left to right)* Robert Holmes Photography; AP/Wide World; David McNew/Liaison Agency

53 Jose Pelaez/Corbis/Stock Market

56 *(top)* Phyllis Picardi/Stock Boston; *(bottom left)* Joseph Nettis/Photo Researchers; *(bottom right)* Lindsay Hebberd/Woodfin Camp

57 *(left to right)* Corbis/Stock Market: Judy Dole/The Image Bank

60 *(left to right, top to bottom)* Botero/J.C. Francolon/Liaison Agency; Poussin/Erich Lessing/Art Resource, NY; Goergia O'Keefe/The Georgia O'Keefe Foundation/Artist's Rights Society (ARS), NY/Art Resource, NY; Christie's London/Superstock; Piet Mondrian, Broadway Boogie Woogie, 1942-43, The Museum of Modern Art, New York. Given anonymously. Photograph © The Museum of Modern Art, 2001; Frida Kahlo, Museo Nacionla de Art Moderno, Mexico, D.F./Art Resource, NY

61 *(left)* Jeff Greenberg/PhotoEdit; *(center left)* Chuck Pefley/Stock Boston; *(center right)* A. Ramey/PhotoEdit; *(right)* Gary Conner/PhotoEdit

63 Photofest

64 George Kerrigan/Digital Eyes

66 *(first row, top to bottom)* David Ball Corbis/Stock Market; Ron Stroud/ Masterfile; Bill Bachman/The Image Works; Steve Benbow/Stock Boston; *(second row, top to bottom)* Sitko/Explorer/Photo Researchers; Lester Lefkowitz/ Corbis/Stock Market; William Katz/Photo Researchers; Tibor Bognar/Corbis/ Stock Market

67 *(top)* Telegraph Color Library/FPG; *(bottom)* Shinichi Kanno/FPG

68 *(left to right, top to bottom)* Robert Oliveri/Liaison Agency; Paramount Pictures/The Everett Collection; Universal Studios/ The Kobal Collection; Paramount Pictures/The Everett Collection

69 *(left to right)* Morgan Creek Product/The Everett Collection; The Everett Collection; Jeff Katz/New Line Cinema/Liaison Agency; Melissa Mosley/ Gramercy Pictures/The Everett Collection

75 *(left & center)* Ron Chapple/FPG; *(right)* L.O.L. Inc./FPG

76 *(top)* P.H. Mcallister/Liaison Agency; *(bottom)* Michael Kevin Daly/ Corbis/Stock Market

77 *(left to right, top to bottom)* courtesy of Polyfoam Concepts USA, Inc.; Courtesy of Hydro Life, Inc.; Courtesy of STL International, Inc.; Kevin Schafer/Stone; Foulon/Leo De Wys

78 *(left)* Will & Deni McIntyre/Stone; *(right)* Joseph Schuyler/Stock Boston

79 FPG

81 *(left & center)* Ron Chapple/FPG; *(right)* Stephen Simpson/FPG

82 *(top)* Sean Cayton/The Image Works; *(right)* David Barber/PhotoEdit

83 *(left to right, top to bottom)* courtesy of Polyfoam Concepts USA, Inc.; Courtesy of Hydro Life, Inc.; Courtesy of STL International, Inc.; Craig Hammell/Corbis/Stock Market; B. Harrington III/Corbis/Stock Market

84 *(left)* Porterfield-Chickering/Photo Researchers; *(right)* Andrea Pistolesi/ The Image Bank

85 The Kobal Collection

87 *(left to right, top to bottom)* courtesy of Polyfoam Concepts USA, Inc.; Courtesy of Hydro Life, Inc.; Courtesy of STL International, Inc.; Photofest